How the Bible Came to Be

Part 1

A Bible Study Series

Through the Bible With

Lance Lambert

How the Bible Came to Be

Part 1

A Bible Study Series

Through the Bible with

Lance Lambert

LANCE LAMBERT MINISTRIES

Richmond, VA

Contents

Introduction

"God, having of old time spoken unto the fathers in the prophets by divers portions and in divers manners, hath at the end of these days spoken unto us in his Son, whom he appointed heir of all things, through whom also he made the worlds; who being the effulgence of his glory, and the very image of his substance, and upholding all things by the word of his power ..." Hebrews 1:1–3a

The Word of God is indeed inspired. This may seem like an obvious statement, yet how often do we consider that the Bible is truly inspired by God? Do we ever take this fact lightly? As you journey through the teachings of Lance, you will gain a fresh new light regarding this fact that Word of God is inspired. Throughout Lance's teachings of the inspiration, authority, theme, aim and scope, structure and growth, and arrangements of the Bible, you will discover how The Lord used men to convey His heart to us in such a timeless way. Just as much for us today just as to those of the days of old. This is no small matter! Yet for the creator of the universe the matter is simple.

As you read through this first volume of the Through the Bible series, you will find a solid case for the authority of the Bible laying a foundation on which your future study through the Bible will be established and solid. Your desire to study the Bible will be drawn out as you read and seek the Lord through his Word. Let's dive into the Word together to see His heart which has been the same from eternity past and will be the same to eternity future.

May He truly continue to reveal Himself to each of us!

1.
The Authority of the Bible

II Timothy 3:14–17

But abide thou in the things which thou hast learned and hast been assured of, knowing of whom thou hast learned them; and that from a babe thou hast known the sacred writings which are able to make thee wise unto salvation through faith which is in Christ Jesus. Every scripture inspired of God is also profitable for teaching, for reproof, for correction, for instruction which is in righteousness: that the man of God may be complete, furnished completely unto every good work.

We are going to deal with this question of the authority of the Bible. There are three words that we generally associate with this subject: authority, revelation, and inspiration. This time we shall confine ourselves more or less to this word authority. Later we will take the other two sides of the matter, revelation and inspiration.

What do we mean by the authority of the Bible? We do not just mean the authority of the translation we may have; we mean the authority and inspiration of the original as it was first spoken and recorded. We will deal another time with the question of whether any mistake or error has come into God's Word as it has been copied and passed down from century to century in its various translations. When we speak of the authority of God's Word, we are speaking of the original form in which God spoke and the way in which it was first actually put down in writing.

What do we mean by the word authority? Why do we speak of the authority of God's Word? We mean that the Scriptures have the power and the right in the hand of God to claim our absolute obedience. That puts the Bible on a footing that no other book, no other writing, no other literature can have. We speak of the authority of the Bible in the sense that we believe it can claim our absolute obedience to every single part. Not only that, we believe it has the right to settle all matters which are in dispute; that is, God's Word is our final court of appeal in the hands of God. From within His Word, we believe that God can settle all matters that are in dispute. In other words, we refuse to accept that God has given us any other standard by which we can judge our affairs or by which we can settle any confusion or dispute or argument that we might have. We believe that God's Word is the final court of appeal. This is what divides us from the Roman Catholic system where the appeal is to the church as well as to the Word of God. In this sense, we believe in the Protestant tradition that God's Word is final and is the highest court of appeal to which we can turn and by which the Holy Spirit can settle all disputes—not the Word of God in the hands of men, but the Word of God in the hands of the Holy Spirit, settling all matters of faith, conduct and order, personal or corporate.

What do we mean by the authority of the Bible? It not only claims our absolute obedience and can settle all our disputes, but it has the right and the power to mould and to fashion our lives, not just in one part of our being, but in every part of our being. In other words, we believe that God's Word has the right to fashion us and mould us. That is why we read the scripture: "Every scripture inspired of God is also profitable for teaching, for reproof, for correction, for instruction which is in righteousness: that the man of God may be complete, furnished completely unto every good work." In other words, God's Word is that we might be complete; there is not anything that God's Word is not able to completely furnish us to do. That is what we mean by the authority of the Bible.

Divine Authorship

The authority of the Bible lies wholly in the fact that it claims divine authorship—not because it happens to be rather wonderful literature, not because it happens to contain some rather remarkable stories, not even because it has the record of the coming into the world of our Lord Jesus Christ. The Bible's claim to authority rests wholly in its claim to divine authorship. It claims to be the Word of the Lord, a divinely self-given revelation, a God-given revelation with power to effect His will in a creative way. In other words, we believe that God's Word is not just a written form of religion. It is not just a code of ethics or some rather interesting bits of history. We believe that in every part, not just in some parts, but in every part, God's Word has a power latent and inherent within it by which it can effect God's will once it is released into the hands of the Holy Spirit in a creative way. In other words, it can create something. Once released, God's Word can create faith in the hearer, not just faith for salvation, but faith to do the works of God. It can create faith to enter into a crucified life. It can create faith to live in the power and enduement of the Holy Spirit. God's Word is in itself powerful, and once it is free in the hands of the Holy Spirit's sovereignty, then God can use it to create something that is absolutely according to His mind.

If those of us who are young in the Lord and those of us who are older in the Lord were to understand what we have got within the Bible, that here is a power that in the hands of the Holy Spirit is unbelievable and incredible, we would reverence it very much more. Not only would we reverence it very much more, but we would be more careful and diligent in our study of it. It would not be just something that we read through early in the morning or late at night before we drop into bed. We would begin to recognize that here within this Book are words which, once in the hands of the Holy Spirit and once we are prepared to be obedient to them, can in fact become a creative power able to effect God's will in us.

However, it is just this that hampers so many of us because the devil's great weapon is unbelief. If he can only get us to read the Bible with an unbelieving heart or some unbelief lurking somewhere, he has got his way—we are reading it like literature. We are reading an historical record. We are reading wonderful doctrine, but inside all the time we are saying it cannot happen; it cannot be; it cannot take place. It is the heart of unbelief that the enemy uses. It is his greatest weapon in the Christian warfare.

Someone once asked Spurgeon to help finance a society for the defence of God's Word and Spurgeon refused to help in any way. He refused to give a penny towards such a society because he said, "God's Word is like a lion. All you have got to do is take it off its chain and it will defend itself." It is absolutely true. God's Word is powerful and living and active. Those are the three words that are always associated with God's Word—powerful, living, active.

Do you and I believe it? The Bible is the Word of God; not just a little bit here and a little bit there that you think is the Word of God. In its entirety, as we have it from beginning to end, from Genesis to Revelation, it is the Word of the Lord, and it is living, powerful, and active. Oh, if only you and I knew it like that. There is a sense in which it is true that God's Word is what we believe it is to us. When we believe that it *can* be and *is* living, powerful, and active, it becomes to us in our personal life living, powerful, and active. When you think it is a dead dog, it becomes a dead dog. That is all. If you merely think, "it is something that is rather wonderful, but ...," it becomes just that to you. The more you prod it, the more dead it will seem to you. The more you turn it over, the more it will seem that you can do anything with it. The more you try to master it, the more it will let you master it. It will not do anything for you. It is when we fully believe the Bible and what it can do in us that we discover it starts to carve us up, master us, and gets a grip on us! We begin to understand that if we will only allow God's Word to do its work, it may be surgical in some cases, but in the end it will always bring us into life and into a large place with the Lord. This Book is the Word of the Lord, and its claim to authority is that it is divinely authorised; it is divinely inspired; it is divinely produced.

The Old Testament Witnesses to the Authority of the Bible

There are three ways, principally, in which we see this claim to authority in the Bible. First of all, in the Old Testament we discover it in the use of these phrases in various ways: "God spake" or "God said" or "the Word of the Lord came" or "thus saith the Lord." One authority says that there are some 3,800 such references.

To these we have to add the acts of God with which the pages of this Book are filled. From the very first chapters of the book of Genesis, right the way through, this Book is crammed not only with the words of God but with the acts of God. In other words, God has spoken in two ways; one is by words and the other is by acts. This Book, being the Word of the Lord, is not just what He said but what He did. For what God has done is as much His Word as what He has said. This Book has a great claim to authority, the Old Testament in particular, in that it claims to contain, not once but thousands of times, whole passages and chapters or more, of what is called the "word that came from the Lord" or "thus saith the Lord" or "God spake." Again, it is the acts of the Lord when He did this or when He did that or when He did the other.

Then we must add to those two categories another, as wonderful if not more wonderful than the other two, and that is the appearances of the Lord. For the Old Testament has not only the words of God, not only the acts of God, but it also has the appearances of God. Not once, but again and again, we discover that God appears. He appears sometimes in a human form, sometimes in the glory, in all kinds of ways. (We cannot stay with that; I am only mentioning these things.) This is the claim of the Old Testament to authority. It is its own claim.

Therefore, if we take these three different categories and bring them together and sum them up it all adds up to one thing—a divinely initiated, a divinely inspired, and a divinely authenticated record or revelation of God. God has revealed Himself by words, by acts, and by appearance.

Christ's witness to the Authority of the Bible

The second claim that we discover in this Book of its absolute and final authority is that Christ Himself witnessed to it. First of all, in John 10:35: "If he called them gods, unto whom the word of God came (and the scripture cannot be broken) ..." It is most interesting that Jesus used two things that explode some theories. He used the first word, "the word of God came," and nearly all theologians would agree that this Book contains God's Word even if they think it is not all God's Word. It is interesting that Jesus goes straight on and says "and the scripture cannot be broken." He equates two things.

Luke 22:37: "For I say unto you, that this which is written must be fulfilled in me, and he was reckoned with transgressors: for that which concerneth me hath fulfilment." Jesus said it must be fulfilled. In one sense, this sums up the attitude of Jesus Himself to the Old Testament. The Scripture cannot be broken; it must be fulfilled.

Matthew 5:17–18: "Think not that I came to destroy the law or the prophets: I came not to destroy, but to fulfil. For verily I say unto you, Till heaven and earth pass away, one jot or one tittle shall in no wise pass away from the law, till all things be accomplished."

Now "the Law" of course is a term that strictly covered the first five books of the Bible, but was also used to cover most if not all of the Old Testament. So Jesus states His faith in that record.

Matthew 22:43: "He saith unto them, How then doth David in the Spirit call him Lord?" Again, these are the words of the Lord Jesus. That is Christ's estimate of the way in which David wrote Psalm 110—in the Spirit. By the way, that also is quoted again in Mark 12.

Then Matthew 19:4–5 "And he [Jesus] answered and said, Have ye not read, that he who made them from the beginning made them male and female, and said, For this cause shall a man leave his father and mother …" Jesus evidently believed that it was God who not only created Adam and Eve but spoke to them.

Matthew 22:31: "But as touching the resurrection of the dead, have ye not read that which was spoken unto you by God, saying …"

Luke 16:16–17: "The law and the prophets were until John: from that time the gospel of the kingdom of God is preached, and every man entereth violently into it. But it is easier for heaven and earth to pass away, than for one tittle of the law to fall."

Luke 18:31: "And he took unto him the twelve, and said unto them, Behold, we go up to Jerusalem, and all the things that are written through the prophets shall be accomplished unto the Son of man."

Luke 24:44–47: "… These are my words which I spake unto you, while I was yet with you, that all things must needs be fulfilled, which are written in the law of Moses, and the prophets, and the psalms, [that is the entirety of the Old Testament] concerning me. Then opened he their mind, that they might understand the scriptures; and he said unto them, Thus it is written, that the Christ should suffer, and rise again from the dead the third day; and that repentance and remission of sins should be preached in his name unto all the nations, beginning from Jerusalem."

When you take all these different scriptures and put them together, you have to come to one conclusion. If you took just one or another on its own you might be able to build a theory on it. But if you bring them all together you must say, if you have an honest and open mind, that Christ obviously, or at least apparently, believed implicitly in the Old Testament. He believed that God spoke there, and that it was divinely inspired. That is quite clear. Many of those who understand their Scriptures the most but would not accept such a conclusion must fall back on other theories that the Lord Jesus just simply adjusted Himself to the theories of His day. Either Christ really did believe fully in the Old Testament as the Word of God or He just simply had to adjust Himself to it and apparently believe it when He knew that a lot of it was not actually so.

However, there is much more. I cannot give you all the scriptures because it would take too much time, but I will just run through a whole list of things that are very interesting. The Lord Jesus Christ believed in Isaiah's authorship. He spoke of Isaiah writing or saying, prophesying in one or two places. He believed in David's authorship of Psalm 110 and says so. He believed in God's creation of Adam and Eve in the beginning. He believed in the history of Cain and Abel. He believed in the history of Noah and the flood, its consequences and the saving of eight people in the ark. Not only that, He believed in the destruction of Sodom and the reason for it. He believed in the turning of Lot's wife into a pillar of salt. He believed in the manna being divinely given from heaven, a miracle given by God the Father. He believed in the brazen serpent and that it was used to heal those who had sinned. He believed in the healing of Naaman, and said so. He believed in the widow of Zarephath and her remarkable deliverance and being kept. He believed in Jonah; not only in the existence of Jonah, but in the fact that Jonah ran away from his divinely ordained task and was swallowed by a sea monster and He says so. He believed also that Jonah was coughed up again onto dry land. These things Christ believed. He did not just say "you have heard the story," but He gave a quite clear indication, at least outwardly, that He believed in the actual historical existence of not only the people but the circumstances that are recorded about them.

There is no doubt that Christ believed implicitly in the authority and the inspiration of the Old Testament. It has been rightly said by someone that the Christian who, in his view of the Bible, stands on any other ground than that on which his Lord stood, does so at his spiritual peril. It is also interesting to underline the claims Christ made for what He said. For instance, He never used the phrase "the word of the Lord came to Me." He never said "thus saith the Lord," although John the Baptist probably did use such phraseology. Instead, Jesus used a completely new and direct approach. He said, "I say unto you." It is most interesting. If you go all the way through the New Testament and underline it, you will find it again and again and again: "they said ... I say unto you," "they said so and so.... I say unto you." He often used this phrase: "verily, verily I say unto you" when He wanted to underline something. In other words, Christ was not only a prophet; He was, in fact, the embodiment of the Word of God. In the Old Testament those who spoke had only been His mouthpiece, as it were. Now He had no need of a mouthpiece because He was not only the Word but the mouthpiece as well.

In John 14:26 He seems to look forward to what we might call the rest of the New Testament, for here we read these words, "But the Comforter, even the Holy Spirit, whom the Father will send in my name, he shall teach you all things, and bring to your remembrance all that I said unto you." It is very interesting that Jesus said that to underline the very writing of the synoptic gospels as well as John and also to infer authority upon what later would be written by the others.

Then again in John 16:12 we read this: "I have yet many things to say unto you, but ye cannot bear them now." Isn't that amazing? He is inferring that He is going to say a good deal more, but He cannot say it now as He is just about to die. Then He goes on, "Howbeit when he, the Spirit of truth, is come, he shall guide you into all the truth: for he shall not speak from himself; but what things soever he shall hear, these shall he speak: and he shall declare unto you the things that are to come" (v. 13). It covers the whole of the New Testament to the book of Revelation. "He shall glorify me: for he shall take of mine, and shall declare it unto you" (v.14). Here we have the second great claim in the Bible to final and absolute authority: the witness of Christ Himself.

The New Testament Witnesses to the Authority of the Bible

The third claim is that the New Testament witnesses to the authority of the Old Testament as well as to its own authority. At the beginning of the New Testament, Matthew 1:22, "Now all this is come to pass, that it might be fulfilled which was spoken by the Lord through the prophet." This is an interesting phrase, and it occurs a number of times in the New Testament: "spoken by the Lord through the prophet."

Matthew 2:15: "... that it might be fulfilled which was spoken by the Lord through the prophet ..."

Acts 1:16: "Brethren, it was needful that the scripture should be fulfilled, which the Holy Spirit spake before by the mouth of David concerning Judas ..." The Holy Spirit spake by the mouth of David. That again is very interesting.

Acts 4:25: "Who by the Holy Spirit, by the mouth of our father David thy servant, didst say ..."

Acts 28:25: "And when they agreed not among themselves, they departed after that Paul had spoken one word, Well spake the Holy Spirit through Isaiah the prophet ..." Here we have some references.

Romans 3:2: "Much every way: first of all, that they [the Jews] were intrusted with the oracles of God."

II Timothy 3:14–17: "But abide thou in the things which thou hast learned and hast been assured of, knowing of whom thou hast learned them; and that from a babe thou hast known the sacred writings which are able to make thee wise unto salvation through faith which is in Christ Jesus. Every scripture inspired of God is also profitable for teaching, for reproof, for correction, for instruction which is in righteousness: that the man of God may be complete, furnished completely unto every good work."

Hebrews 1:5–8: We will not read it all, but I want to point out to you here that between verses 5, 8, and 13 and all of the last part of chapter 1, there are seven different quotations of various parts of the Old Testament. Every one of them begins with this: "For unto which of the angels said He [God] at any time, Thou art ..." Again in verse 7: "And of the angels [God] saith ..." Verse 13: "But of which of the angels hath he [God] said at any time ..." Again there is a claim that God spake all of this. God was the author of it all, although we know that many of them are by different human agents.

Hebrews 2:2: "For if the word spoken through angels proved stedfast ..."

Verse 3: "How shall we escape, if we neglect so great a salvation? which having at the first been spoken through the Lord, was confirmed unto us by them that heard." You have the whole Bible there—Old and New Testament. Thus, the Lord is behind it all; God is behind it all, speaking in the beginning through angels, then through the Lord, and then to them who confirmed it.

Hebrews 3:7: "Wherefore, even as the Holy Spirit saith, Today if ye shall hear his voice harden not your hearts ..."

Hebrews 4:4: "For He [God] hath said ..." This is about another part which we know to be written by Moses. It is very interesting because it is history and not an actual quotation of what God said.

Then again, you will find Hebrews 12:25–26. It is another claim of God speaking.

1 Peter 1:10–12a: "Concerning which salvation the prophets sought and searched diligently, who prophesied of the grace that should come unto you: searching what time or what manner of time the Spirit of Christ which was in them did point unto, when it testified beforehand the sufferings of Christ, and the glories that should follow them. To whom it was revealed, that not unto themselves, but unto you, did they minister these things, which now have been announced unto you through them that preached the gospel ..."

Here we have a claim that it was the Holy Spirit who was in the prophets. The word prophets here does not simply mean the actual technical section of the Old Testament which we call the prophets, but covers the much larger realm including Moses and many others who in the Scriptures are termed prophets.

II Peter 1:21: "For no prophecy ever came by the will of man: but men spake from God, being moved by the Holy Spirit." That covers a very large section of the Old Testament.

I know this is a lot of references, but people speak so glibly and so lightly when challenged in their offices and by other people how they believe in God's Word, and they cannot give any reason why they do. People think that you are just credulous and a bit woolly headed, and not to say the least, probably very simple minded! It is very good to know upon what your faith really rests.

Now, I want you to note two special references. Romans 15:4 is a very interesting verse: "For whatsoever things were written aforetime were written for our learning, that through patience and through comfort of the scriptures we might have hope." This is a very comprehensive verse: "Whatsoever things were written before time were written for our learning." Very interesting.

I Corinthians 10:11: "Now these things happened unto them by way of example; and they were written for our admonition, upon whom the ends of the ages are come." These are two very interesting verses which cover a very large part of the Old Testament, if not all of it.

We have covered the New Testament and some of the scriptures that witness to the authority of the Old Testament. Now, does the New Testament witness to its own authority? I have already shown you some of the things that Christ said. His claims were absolutely direct and dogmatic, and we will leave that.

I Corinthians 14:37: "If any man thinketh himself to be a prophet, or spiritual, let him take knowledge of the things which I write unto you, that they are the commandment of the Lord." That is interesting because it comes at the end of this whole letter in which there are many, many things written.

I Thessalonians 2:13: "And for this cause we also thank God without ceasing, that, when ye received from us the word of the message, even the word of God, ye accepted it not as the word of men, but, as it is in truth, the word of God, which also worketh in you that believe." They believed that their word, not only which they spoke, but the word which they wrote was in fact the Word of God.

This next verse is one that I find the most interesting of all. It is the kind of verse that you gloss over when you are reading and do not really take full note of it.

II Peter 3:16: "As also in all his epistles, speaking in them of these things; wherein are some things hard to be understood, which the ignorant and unstedfast wrest, as they do also the other scriptures, unto their own destruction."

That is the most amazing thing for the apostle Peter to write. He actually looked upon the epistles of Paul as Scripture. In Paul and Peter's own lifetime, he looked upon the letters of Paul as Scripture, and it is referred here as "also the other scriptures." It does not say, "as also the scriptures," but "as also the other scriptures." That is interesting because it shows that toward the end of Paul and Peter's ministry they had already begun to recognize that what was being written down of their message was the Word of God. It was already forming into the conclusion of the Old Testament.

When you bring all of this together, it is a wealth of evidence for a claim to divine authorship. You cannot get over it; you cannot just dissect it. In fact, you get into more trouble that way. The whole point is that when you take the Bible as a whole, Old Testament and

New Testament there is this three-fold claim to divine authorship. In the Old Testament within itself, Christ's witness to it and to what He was saying as well as to what was to come, and also the New Testament witness to the authority of the Old as well as to its own authority.

It is very interesting that the book of Revelation was one of the most contested pieces of Scripture, and in the fourth century it was still not completely and universally recognized as part of the canon of Scripture. However, when you read the last chapter of Revelation, it ends up with these words in its final place to which now universal recognition is given to it: "I testify unto every man that heareth the words of the prophecy of this book, If any man shall add unto them, God shall add unto him the plagues which are written in this book: and if any man shall take away from the words of the book of this prophecy, God shall take away his part from the tree of life, and out of the holy city, which are written in this book" (Revelation 22:18–19). These are sobering words. Of course, primarily they speak of the actual book of Revelation, but it is interesting that they are amongst the closing words of this whole record, this revelation of God.

The Holy Spirit's Witness to the Authority of the Bible

Now, those are three claims that are clear within the Bible itself. There are also some other ways in which this claim is supported. I want to dwell on those other ways that the claim to final authority is supported. First, and here is a very interesting fact: whenever and wherever the Holy Spirit is sovereign and free, He unfailingly witnesses to the absolute authority and inspiration of the Bible.

This is a remarkable fact in both persons and movements. If you look into church history you will have to look a long, long way to find any man (if you can find one) in whom the Holy Spirit was sovereign and free who did not recognize the authority and inspiration of God's Word, going right back to the church fathers. It is a most remarkable fact. Of course, we can say many other things about this, but we must say straightaway that as soon as a movement begins to depart from this foundation of the authority and inspiration of God's Word, it loses its spiritual character.

Church history is strewn with such monuments of things, which were begun by the Holy Spirit, which gave unfailing allegiance, not only to the Lord Jesus Christ, His divinity and to orthodox doctrine, but also to the authority and inspiration of God's Word. Then, gradually the shift of emphasis came, and slowly but surely, they departed and became their own prophet societies. They become just simply movements out of which the spiritual fire and the spiritual character have long since departed. I am not saying that you will not find true Christians in such; you do. What I am saying is that when the Holy Spirit is sovereign and free, He seems to witness to the authority of God's Word. However, when He is no longer sovereign and no longer free, the authority of God's Word is one of the first things to be jettisoned. That is a fact.

Another fact, which is very interesting in support of this claim, is the matter of fulfilled prophecy. I do not think there is any more fascinating subject in the whole of the Bible than the matter of fulfilled prophecy. It does not matter if it is messianic, that is, prophesies of Christ which have been fulfilled, or whether it is otherwise—prophesies concerning Egypt, or Assyria, or Persia, or Greece and Rome. All these things which have been fulfilled are in themselves the most remarkable evidence for divine authorship.

You see, it is interesting that in the book of Deuteronomy God says that one of the evidences of the source of a thing being divine is whether what is said is fulfilled. It is certainly true that the Bible within itself gives plenty of evidence, if that is a basis, for it being divinely produced. I could give many examples, but this is the kind of thing with which we could get side-tracked because we could literally spend hours on the question of fulfilled prophecy.

Fulfilled Prophecy Concerning Christ

Just consider the Lord Jesus Christ. In Isaiah 7:14 we are told that He would be born of a young woman or a virgin (the word can mean either), and His name will be called Emmanuel. Someone may say that is obscure. We know that He was born of a virgin, but it is a bit obscure.

As we go on, there is an amazing reference in Isaiah 9 to Galilee of the nations—despised Galilee. It tells us that a light is going to come out of Galilee which is going to enlighten the nations. The most remarkable thing is that he goes on: "Unto us a son is born, unto us a child is given." It is Christ.

Then we come to Micah 5:2, and there is an amazing reference to Bethlehem Ephrathah: "But thou, Bethlehem Ephrathah, which art little to be among the thousands of Judah, out of thee shall one come forth unto me that is to be ruler in Israel; whose goings forth are from of old, from everlasting." This is a most remarkable prophecy of Someone who is not just human, but Someone who has His being in past eternity. He will come into Bethlehem, and will come out of Bethlehem. This Man, it says, shall be our peace. This Man shall be our peace! The thought is blasphemy; yet that prophecy was remarkably fulfilled when Christ was born in Bethlehem. The one who comes out of Galilee was remarkably fulfilled when He was brought up in Nazareth in Galilee where He spent the first thirty years of His life.

A person may say he cannot quite accept that, but what about Zechariah's prophecy about Christ coming to Jerusalem, into Zion, lowly, riding upon a colt the foal of an ass? (see 9:9) It has been remarkably fulfilled. Someone may say straightaway, "Just wait, perhaps the Lord Jesus knew that prophecy." Well, He must have been remarkable if He knew that prophecy and scanned all the way through the whole of the Old Testament, because to many of us it would be obscure if we did not know that He had actually fulfilled it. Yet, there it stands in the middle of the passage concerning the coming Messiah. It says that when He finally comes in triumph into Jerusalem, He will come riding on a colt, the foal of an ass. And everyone will cry, "Hosanna!" Yes, fulfilled! Yet a little farther on you discover there are marks in His hands. He's been wounded in the house of His friends. We are told that a fountain is to be opened for the uncleanness of the house of David where it can be washed away. There is prophecy fulfilled!

Someone will say that they still cannot believe; so let me take you then to Isaiah 53. Is there any more remarkable prophecy in the whole of Scripture? "He was wounded for our transgressions, he was bruised for our iniquities; the chastisement of our peace fell upon him; and with his stripes we are healed. All we like sheep have gone astray; we have turned every one to his own way; and Jehovah hath laid on him the iniquity of us all" (vv. 5–6).

Listen; carry yourself back into the Old Testament. What is Isaiah talking about? Where is this conception of the Messiah as one of absolute majesty and power in the eyes and minds of the whole nation? They longed for the day when their great deliverer would come and lead the armies of the children of God into possession of the Promised Land. He was going to be one greater than Solomon. Oh yes, that is the kind of man they looked for. Here you get Isaiah. Who could he be talking about? Was he talking about himself? Was he talking about some other person in his day? Who was he referring to? "He was wounded for our transgression. He was bruised for our iniquities." What is in his mind? There is only one explanation. It was the Spirit of Christ that put it in him, testifying beforehand unto the sufferings of Christ. It is the only way. Is there any other explanation?

Go on in that marvellous chapter where it says, "they made His grave with the wicked, and with a rich man in His death" (v. 9). It is an absolute eyewitness account of Calvary. There He is between two thieves; He is numbered amongst the transgressors. There He is buried in a rich man's tomb. Who could have thought it out? No wonder two hundred years ago people were convinced that that portion of Isaiah had been written-in after Calvary. I do not wonder at it! It is almost an eyewitness account, not only of what happened at Calvary but of New Testament doctrine.

Oh, some would say, "You do not convince me; I am awfully sorry." I take you then to Psalm 22. This is King David and it opens with this cry: "My God, my God, why hast Thou forsaken me? Why art Thou so far from helping me?" Read through the Psalm. It is an eyewitness account! Where is it coming from? This time it is not an eyewitness account of someone standing in the crowd watching the cross; it is an eyewitness account from the cross itself looking down at the people. There within the crucified form of Christ you are looking out of His eyes and you see the people. "They are gaping at Me." Listen to them! They cry out, "Come down! He trusted in God; let God save Him if He thinks He is the darling of God." Then He looks down to the foot of the cross and says, "They divided My garments and cast lots for My coat. They pierced My hands and feet." Even when He is dead, it is still as if you are looking at it from His eyes. They did not break any of His bones; all His bones were kept.

How did that Psalm get written? What experience was David going through that he could write such a thing? It is not true of David. He never had an experience like that! Read it. No, the answer is this: it was the Spirit of Christ in David testifying to the sufferings of Christ.

I have only given you a few of the prophecies that have been fulfilled, and I could go on and on. You can see why the Lord Jesus was so absolutely convinced that not one jot or one tittle of the Law would pass away till all these things be fulfilled. My dear friend, there are a lot more things that are yet to be fulfilled and there is not going to be one jot or one tittle of it that will pass away till everything has been fulfilled. Just as it has been, so it will be. That is our absolute faith in the authority of God's Word.

I could tell you about Daniel, chapters 2 and 7. There you have the most amazing portrayal of the times of the Gentiles from Babylon right down to our own day, every bit of it being fulfilled, except the last part, when finally the whole thing will be destroyed by the emergence from heaven of the stone not cut with hands. That is Christ—everything fulfilled.

The Unity of the Bible

The third thing that supports the claim of divine authority is the unity of the Bible. The Bible has sixty-six books, thirty-nine Old and twenty-seven New. It has different human authors with different backgrounds, who lived in different times. Even their languages were different in some cases. Yet there is only one theme that runs throughout from beginning to end. The whole Bible, from Genesis to Revelation, is woven together into one great theme and it is woven together without any editorial committee whatsoever at any time. This is within itself one of the most remarkable evidences for divine authorship and therefore for the authority of the Bible. When you go right back to the beginning with Moses and then go right forward to the end with the apostle John, you have two men who lived at very different times, passing by thousands of years, whose backgrounds were different, whose way of life was different, yet somehow or another, they correspond. Did they know they were corresponding? Did John make a careful study of the Old Testament and then sit down and write so that he actually concluded it? I believe that it is beyond the powers of the human mind to have done it. There is so much that is obviously unsuspecting, which is a conclusion of what has gone before.

This unity is even more remarkable when you get men like Job and women like Ruth and others who obviously had nothing to do with each other. You have the Song of Solomon, by whoever wrote it, Solomon or someone else, and you have another book, shall we say like Hosea. None of these knew each other; they had different backgrounds, they lived at different times, yet they had a theme. The interesting thing is that these men probably could not even read what the others had said. Some of the material had not even been collected together; yet somehow there is a thread that runs through it all.

The Types in Scripture

The unity is not just in a few things; it is in all kinds of things. For instance, there are types in Scripture; you find the dove as well as the raven are the same from beginning to end. There is the olive tree, the fig tree, and the vine. Many different things from beginning to end run right the way through and have the same symbolic meaning. Of course, someone can argue that this may have been known and that symbolism may have been used. That is true; nevertheless, there is much else that is quite remarkable.

When you consider the matter of the cherubim, you find that Ezekiel borrows a tremendous amount from Babylon when he writes about the cherubim. It is not that he just borrows something from heathen and pagan sources, but he brings the whole matter of the cherubim onto another level. He does not depart from the original; he adds to it and develops it. Then we begin to see something that we had never seen before so that without Ezekiel we could not understand the cherubim. When we come to John the apostle, he does not know anything about Babylon except that it is a symbol of the world. His description of the cherubim is not the same as Ezekiel, and yet it corresponds. So we could go on and on.

The Bible is a unity from beginning to end. It is interesting that all the books came together slowly. They were recognized bit by bit, part by part, until finally we have what we call the Scriptures. I had mentioned a little earlier that the book of Revelation was one of the last pieces of the Bible to be finally and universally recognized as canonical. That is true, yet none of us would now question the book of Revelation; we see it as an absolute conclusion to the rest of the Bible. It is the topstone. Without it, much would be unfinished and unconcluded, yet here we have it all in the book of Revelation. It was not that some committee got together and finally decided. There was a long, long battle until there was universal recognition, and finally it slipped into its rightful place.

I have often spoken to you about Genesis, chapters 1, 2, and 3, and Revelation, chapters 20, 21, and 22, and how those three chapters at the beginning and three at the end completely correspond. That within itself is absolutely remarkable. The interesting thing is that in John's day he never knew that the book of Revelation that he had written down would be the final word of the Bible. Many centuries after he was dead and gone it finally came to its place at the end of the Bible. That is the interesting thing. If there was any collection of things in John's day, it was quite different from what we have now. The thing that is so utterly interesting is that John's revelation is now in its right place and he was not the one who got it there. That is the point. If he had sat down and said, "Now look, I am going to write a conclusion to the Bible. I am going to conclude the whole thing so that the whole of it is clear to everyone." He was an apostle; the Lord could have said to him: "Now look here, you must see that all this gets into its right place." He never did anything of the kind. John wrote it down; he knew it was the Word of God, and he left it to the Holy Spirit. After centuries of conflict, finally it came into its rightful place. I leave that with you, as well as whatever else we could say about that.

The Power Inherent Within Scripture

Another thing that we must say in support of this divine authorship and therefore the authority of the Bible is the amazing power inherent within Scripture in all its parts. It has an inherent power to speak. Have you ever had the Bible speak to you? Have you ever had an obscure bit of the book of Job leap out of the text and almost hit you between the eyes? Have you ever had a part of the story in Judges just come out to you as if God is actually defining to you the circumstances in which you live and was actually telling you what to do? Have you ever read some part of I Chronicles, that you never thought even existed, and all of a sudden seen something? That is what I am talking about. It is not only the Sermon on the Mount or only I Corinthians 13 or Isaiah 43, which is beloved of all dear and old Christians. No, it is not just those well-worn parts of the Bible. I am talking about parts of the Bible which sometimes seem to have little to say, yet when you are in a time of trouble it is a strange thing how an obscure bit of the Scripture that you have never read, or if you had read it you had never thought about it, comes right out and leaps at you, and you live on it. If you believe it, it becomes living, powerful, and active, and it does something in you.

Why does the Bible do that? The interesting thing is that you can go right back to the days of the Psalmist and you will find that all of them have a common experience, Old Testament and New Testament. All of us have a common experience—the Bible lives to us. It is the Word of God to us. It comes alive to us. When we are in trouble we call to the Lord and He hears us; He speaks to us. What is this thing that binds us all together? We have different languages, different backgrounds, and even different ages; yet we have all found that God's Word is not just literature or just a book.

Why don't the wonderful works of Shakespeare—so wonderful in themselves, so telling—why don't they leap out like that? They have a lot to say sometimes about human situations (for those of you who read Shakespeare), but it is not the same as Scripture. It does not come out at you in the same way. There are things that make you think: "How clever! What a genius! How did he do that? What an insight into human nature!" The Bible is different however. It not only has insight into human nature, it not only has divine genius behind it, it has so much more. Somehow or other it talks to our heart and explains things to us. It gets into us and does something for us. We can be absolutely down and suddenly God's Word comes to us and we are up; we are out. However, it is not only when we are depressed and things like that. God's Word has meant life for some people on beds of sickness. A Word of God has come in and they have gotten up and never got down in that bed of sickness again. There are some people who have had other troubles and the Word of the Lord has come to them, and suddenly they have taken that Word for themselves.

I know there is a lot that is fraudulent and a lot that is hypocritical and there is a facade about many Christian lives, but there is also a lot that is genuine. There are those who know the Word of God and the Word of God has gotten into them. They have found that the Word of God has an amazing power inherent within it to speak, to change, to convict, and to comfort. It can create faith in us when we are faithless. Have you ever known that period of absolute darkness when there is not a flicker of faith? Then suddenly the word of the

Lord comes to you and something just weakly but deliberately takes hold of it and faith comes? Then you are out. I have known it again and again in just material provision. I had thought the Lord would never, ever provide on this, or never, ever provide on that, and darkness was coming in. Then a word of the Lord has come; and something flickers within and says, "Oh yes, He will. Yes, He will!" You then take hold of God's word and God has done it.

God's Word is so contemporary. Dear old Job would have a fit if we could take him down to Piccadilly today, if we took him to a London airport and he saw those great big things taking off. Poor Job would not know if he was on his head or his feet! He would be flabbergasted. Yet, Job has written things from his day, when the mode of transport was a camel and hardly anything else was known, which is as contemporary as anything in the newspaper today. It can get right into my contemporary situation and speak contemporary language to me. That is the whole point. I do not know if any of you have ever had God speak to you from Genesis 1 or 2, but I have. He has spoken to me about a contemporary situation in a very contemporary way from an uncontemporary chapter of the Bible. That is God's Word. It is living. In other words, it is not dead. It is not historic, not yesterday. It is today and it is living! So, in a sense, all of God's Word has something to say in today's time, even in the most obscure parts, but that again we must leave.

The Well-being of Believers

Then there is another sobering fact, which supports the claim to the authority of God's Word. It is rather negative, but it is a fact. As soon as a man begins to question the authority and inspiration of God's Word, as soon as he begins to belittle its power, as soon as he takes a superior position to it, that one, whether man or woman, opens the floodgate of doubt and unbelief, and before very long, he loses his joy, his peace, his confidence, and his spiritual life.

In my life—I have been saved for about twenty years—I have seen two things. I have seen a number of people who had liberal or unsound views of the Scripture move from that view to a complete and utter faith in the authority and inspiration of God's Word. Always I have seen the same thing. I have seen them get peace and joy; I have seen their lives become full of faith and I've seen them growing in Christ. However, I have also seen people do the opposite. They move from a complete confidence in the authority of God's Word onto an unsure basis where they are not sure, where they doubt, where they question. I have seen exactly the same— spiritual deterioration. Why? That is the point. There is a point and it is a big point; it is a factor. There is something about the authority of God's Word that is absolutely fundamental to the well-being of our spiritual life.

In II Peter 3:16 it speaks of people who are ignorant and unstable, and it does not just mean simple-minded. It means spiritually ignorant and spiritually unstable. They wrest these things to their own destruction. There were some men in Paul's day who were teachers of God's Word and evidently had a standard of intelligence and spiritual character as well, but they got into trouble. Paul said that they had made spiritual shipwreck (see I Timothy 1:19). It is interesting, isn't it?

The Endurance of God's Word

Here is another amazing thing about God's Word. God's Word as we now have it has endured millenniums of opposition and antagonism. Not only that, there has been sheer carelessness in many cases. When you think of just the Old Testament and that it came through Egypt. How did we get it? Why was it not destroyed? How have we gotten it in the way we have got it now? People start talking about bits and pieces being missing, but look at what we have got! That is the amazing thing! When you think of it going into Egypt and then coming out of Egypt, going through forty years in the wilderness and then into the Promised Land—it could have so easily been completely mutilated. Where are the other records that we have of ancient writings? Half of them are mutilated, but the Bible has come through to us, in a sense, in the most remarkable way. As far as God is concerned, a lot of it may be missing that was originally there; I don't know, but I do know that what God intended obviously is here. There is a complete theme or unity running through it all. It is remarkable, isn't it? All that we need is in this Book, and that is the point. Maybe bits and pieces have dropped out, but what does it matter? The point is that all we need is here, and it is not in Egypt—all those years, all those centuries of trouble and difficulty and so on, within the land. What about the Assyrian exile? What about the Babylonian exile? The whole lot was destroyed and all the archives were completely burned. The whole thing was finished. We have very little of Jewish history because it was all destroyed in the Assyrian sieges, the Babylonian siege, and the Roman conquest, but we have all that we need in the Bible.

That is amazing! We could go on and on and on because it really is quite remarkable.

When you go through the persecutions and see the way Christian writings were destroyed in persecution after persecution, you realise that somehow or other God has preserved something. He has supernaturally preserved the record. I suggest that if you want to read the story direct, read F.F. Bruce and a few of the others who have written accounts on the way we have gotten the Bible. It is amazing.

Not only that, think of the men who have died to give us this Book, people who died in flames and in dungeons only to give us this Book. It was not that we might take superior positions, not that we might belittle it, not that we might just feel that it is not really so much. Those men gave their lives because they believed that this Book in its entirety was the Word of God and was worth dying for in order to let us have it. They died. We have got the Book and it is free.

The Bible in Translation

There is something else that we ought to remember and it is that we have the Bible in translation. It is an amazing thing! There are very few people who could read the Bible in its original language. We have got it in translation in most every nation of the world, and it is the same Word of God in every nation—powerful, living, active and able to do the same work.

What book could be so translated? I know because I had to study the scriptures of the Buddhist, Taoist, Confucian, and Shintoist sects. I can only say that though I myself reverenced some of those scriptures, not as divinely inspired but as a result of a real quest after God, containing real wisdom in many cases, yet it is not true that they come anywhere near God's Word. I know the difference, and I think you would too.

We are bound therefore to say, as in all other essential matters—in the question of our salvation, in the question of what the church is, in the question of what the purpose of God is, that God is absolute. He has defined it clearly from beginning to end. It is the same with His Word. He has not left us to decide what is His Word. He has given it to us, clearly defined from beginning to end. We are now to accept it by faith. He has not left it to the tender mercies of our own judgment and discretion. God has clearly defined what He has given to us. He gives it to us to be received through faith.

There are things which are difficult to understand. There are things that are hard to reconcile with other things in the Bible, and there are some things that seem incompatible with God. Those things we will admit, and we will seek to deal with them later on. We expect difficulties when the finite is dealing with the infinite, when the imperfect comes to deal with the perfect, when the ignorant (relatively speaking) comes to deal with the all-wise—wisdom personified. We expect difficulties; we cannot tie up everything. We are created and God is the Creator. The amazing thing is that God, in the compass of a small volume, has in weak, human language expressed a vast and endless universe of inexhaustible wisdom. You and I will never come to the end of it. Men have been studying this Book for centuries upon centuries and have not come to the end of it. They have not plumbed its depths. No wonder Paul gets lost in it and talks about the depths of the riches of the wisdom and the knowledge of God. You are lost in this Book. It is not just an ordinary book. It is quite remarkable and it is all contained in that Book. Only God could have done it; to put something within those pages which no human mind has yet fully mastered; yet those who have tried to master it have shipwrecked themselves.

Here we have something that I believe must speak to us. Once we believe what God has put within the compass of this one volume, if we trust it and obey it, we shall discover it powerful enough to change not only individuals, not only nations, but history itself. The Bible is one of the most remarkable things in the whole history of the human race. Should there be anyone who still doubts whether God could have so spoken to man, then I must ask you whether God is God? If God is God, then it is possible. It is gloriously possible! If He has done it, then the requirement is reverent faith, honest inquiry, and true humility as we approach this Book.

Thus, you see that Scripture is given to us that we might be furnished completely. We see the supreme authority of the Word of God, and it is like an act of Parliament—operative and authoritative to the last and farthest extremity of its letter.

2.
Revelation

We come to the second part of the three-fold inquiry into the nature of God's Word. We have been considering together about the authority of God's Word, and now we are going to consider this matter of revelation. What is revelation, the revelation that is contained in God's Word or more correctly the revelation that is the Bible? These matters are absolutely fundamental to our spiritual well-being.

What do we mean by the word *revelation*? It is a word that we use a lot, "to reveal." We often ask for a spiritual revelation to be given to us or we ask that a thing may be revealed to us. In a much bigger way we speak of the term revelation, meaning the revelation of God and of His ways that is in the Bible.

The *Oxford Dictionary* gives this definition: "Revelation is the disclosing of knowledge to man by divine or supernatural agency." The idea is that something which is hidden, which is obscure, which is, as it were, in the dark is suddenly made manifest. It is brought out into the light and made clear; it is suddenly revealed or expressed. Both the Hebrew and the Greek words which are translated in the Bible by this word *revelation* or to *reveal* mean the same thing: "to uncover or to unveil." The idea behind this word revelation is something that was covered up but is now uncovered or something which was veiled before is now unveiled. The very word *revelation* means, "to draw aside the curtain." In Luke 10:21 you have the two words which are opposite: "O Father, Lord of heaven and earth, that Thou didst hide these things from the wise and understanding ..." That is one side; it has been hidden from the wise and understanding. On the other side we read: "And thou didst reveal them unto babes." These things are veiled to the wise and understanding but unveiled to the babes. They are covered before the sight of those with great, natural intellect and intelligence and uncovered where there is humility and dependence upon the Lord.

The Bible is therefore the revelation or the unveiling or the uncovering of God Himself. God has used this term with the idea that He has been covered, hidden, veiled, and it was impossible for man to penetrate that veil, that covering, but God has now uncovered or unveiled Himself. That is exactly what the Bible claims to be: the unveiling of God Himself, given by inspiration of the Holy Spirit through certain men, to man. It is the unveiling of God's heart and God's mind, but it is also the unveiling of God's purpose and of His salvation. In other words, the compass of this revelation is that God has uncovered His heart. He has laid bare Himself to man, and not only Himself but His purpose from the beginning, from eternity to eternity. Not only that, He has revealed the way by which sinful and worthless men and women can, through His grace, become incorporated into Himself. They can become partakers of His own life and nature and by so doing can become once more heirs of the purpose of God. This is what the Bible is. It is an authoritative and unique revelation.

Revelation of the Word of God

Now, what the human mind and intellect could never attain to naturally, what was beyond man's ability to discover by himself, God has chosen to reveal. The apostle Paul says, "What was beyond our seeing, things beyond our hearing and beyond our imagining are all prepared by God for those who love Him. These are revealed by God to us through His Spirit" (see 1 Corinthians 2:9–10). There is a whole realm that is impossible for natural man to penetrate, to explore; a whole realm in which the greatest of human intellects become folly. They trip up, they become confused and bewildered and lost. It is impossible to discover naturally what God is, what His purpose is, and what He claims to be doing. But God has revealed it, and this revelation is what we call the Bible. This unveiling of God Himself is in fact a progressive revelation. God has not just suddenly given one part, as it were, that is absolutely final. No, in God's wisdom He began in a quiet way, and gradually down through the centuries He has unfolded His purpose. He has laid bare more and more fully His heart until finally we come to the great climax in the Person of the Lord Jesus Christ. God has laid His heart as fully bare as He is able to do so in Him.

A Progressive Revelation

The Bible begins with Genesis and it progresses and develops all the way through, unfolding more and more fully until you come to the book of Revelation where it finishes. It is important for us to understand that this revelation is a progressive revelation and it is only when we come to the end of the Bible that we really have got something more full and complete. In other words, it is like a huge river; there are lots and lots of tributaries, little rivulets and streamlets that run down into it, gradually forming one huge torrent, until finally it runs out into the ocean. This is just like God's Word. You begin, as it were, in the book of Genesis with just a small idea about something. Things are not explained; they are just stated. Facts are given to you that have caused a lot of concern, discussion and controversy. There are facts about this, facts about that, but a few things are clearly stated without a lot of explanation. There is some explanation especially as to the nature of man, the origin of man and God's intention in man, his constitution, but the rest is not explained or interpreted. Then, as you go on you get another little rivulet that comes in of understanding and then a little farther along another, and then as you move on you come to the prophets and there is more light thrown upon things.

For instance, let's take as an example the introduction of the serpent in the third chapter of the book of Genesis. We are not told anything about the serpent. If you only had the first three chapters of Genesis you would wonder what this is all about. Who is this serpent? Who is this creature that can speak and evidently is the great adversary of God? Who is he? But it is right in the book of Ezekiel and the book of Isaiah. These two prophets begin to explain to us a little more of what lies behind that picture, that story that we get in the garden. So you understand what I mean by progressive revelation.

We have the bare facts stated that God has a great archenemy, a great adversary, and he has come into the garden and has sought to withstand God and to wreck God's purpose. Indeed, it would seem that he has achieved His objective and everything has fallen into ruin. However, as you go on, you begin to find a little more is explained, and a little more is explained, and a little more is explained, and we begin to discover that this person in the garden is not just a serpent. There is much more to him than that. He may have a serpent-like nature, but we discover that he was one of the great angels of God, *the* great archangel of God—Lucifer, the son of light. Then we begin to discover that he occupied a position with God which was almost unique amongst the angels. Then we find that something went wrong and somehow or other trouble came in. It is only when you get to the book of Revelation at the end of the Bible that you discover it was a third of the angels of heaven that were involved in this rebellion. It is in the New Testament that you discover that this one we are talking about is called "the prince of this world." Even the Lord Jesus does not gainsay his authority. He calls him "the prince of this world." When the devil said to the Lord Jesus: "Worship me and I will give You all the kingdoms of the world," the Lord Jesus did not say to him, "you are a liar; you cannot give Me the kingdoms of the world." He never for one moment sought to discuss it or argue with him as if the Lord knew because He calls him the prince of this world, one who has great authority and power in the world. That is what we mean by progressive revelation.

In Hebrews 1:1–2a: "God, having of old time spoken unto the fathers in the prophets by divers portions and in divers manners, hath at the end of these days spoken unto us in his Son."

Now mark the word portions and manners. "Hath in divers portions and in divers manners" (ASV). Darby has translated it like this: "Hath in many parts and in many ways spoken unto us in the prophets." The New English Bible puts it: "Hath in many fragmentary and various ways spoken unto us in the prophets."

The revelation contained in the Old Testament right up to the coming of Christ is in various ways, by various methods, and in various phases. In other words, God has used all kinds of methods to reveal Himself. Not only has He used all kinds of methods, but He has had, as it were, certain phases. The revelation has been fragmentary; it has been given first this, then that, and then the other; until when you come to the New Testament, all the pieces of the jigsaw begin to fit together, and you begin to see for the first time the picture as it is intended to be. I believe that is important.

Revelation Through Direct Speech

This revelation is given, as we have said, through many different methods in different phases. How is it given? There are a number of ways by which God has revealed Himself as we find in the Bible. I can only give you one or two examples of each of these ways, and there are many others of course. God has revealed Himself firstly through direct speech. An example of that is in Exodus 20:1: "And God spake all these words, saying ..." We are told a little later on that He wrote these words, the Ten Commandments with His finger. They were written with the finger of God in stone by direct speech. Now this is not just one isolated instance. There are a large, large number of such instances where God revealed Himself by direct speech. He revealed Himself to the prophets and said, "I Am so and so and so and so," not only to the patriarchs but later to the prophets by direct speech.

Revelation Through Prophecy

Another way that God has revealed Himself is through prophecy. An example of that is in Isaiah 53. We all know this great chapter about the suffering and atoning death of the Lord Jesus Christ. But you will see in chapter 52:3, all of which is part of the same passage, these words: "For thus saith the Lord ..." The Lord is here speaking by prophecy. Again, verse 13 is the Lord speaking in the prophet: "Behold, my servant ..." Isaiah was not speaking of some servant of his; he was speaking in the Spirit. The Spirit of God was speaking in Isaiah; thus it was God who was speaking. Only this time it was not just God speaking to Isaiah; it was God speaking in Isaiah out of him. "Behold, my servant shall prosper ..." Now that is the way he introduces this tremendous prophecy of the suffering Servant, the Lord Jesus Christ. There is a tremendous amount of prophecy in the Bible.

Revelation Through History

There is another way that God has revealed Himself in the Bible, and that is through history. Now when I use the word *history* I not only mean corporate or national history but personal history. That is why I think it is best to include the word *history* and *experience*. And I include in that not only just the ordinary record of history, the wanderings of Abraham and so on, but also all the miraculous events that are recorded in God's Word.

For example, in Exodus 13 and 14 we have the story of the Passover and the Exodus. This is history recorded by the Holy Spirit.

Whatever others might say, this is sacred history. It is the record of what God told His people to do, how they did it, how they were saved from the death of the first born, and then how they went through the Red Sea and over into the wilderness. They should have gone on to the Promised Land. God revealed Himself through the Passover and He revealed Himself through the Exodus, and this two-fold event underlies nearly the whole Bible. From this point onwards, the Passover and the Exodus are the most fundamental things in the Bible. There is no getting away from it. Everything goes back to the Passover and everything goes back to the deliverance through the Red Sea. Jesus spoke of His death as being directly connected with the Passover and the Exodus. He spoke of His decease, which would be accomplished at Jerusalem, and the word He used for the "decease" was the word exodus. He spoke of His exodus which would be accomplished at Jerusalem. He saw Calvary as the great Passover of world history by which multitudes would be delivered. He saw His death and resurrection as the exodus by which people would be taken out of Egypt and into the Promised Land. I only give you this as an example. All the prophets go back to the Passover. Every great national recovery began with the restoration and keeping of the Passover. We could go on and on.

Revelation Through Experience

God has not only revealed Himself through history but also experience. Take for instance, the Psalms. How has God revealed Himself in the Psalms? God reveals His heart and His ways in the Psalms perhaps more than most of the books of the Old Testament. And how? He has revealed Himself through the experiences of the Psalmist so that when the Psalmist speaks of things like "Hope thou in God; for I shall yet praise him, who is the help of my countenance, and my God" (Psalm 43:5b), that speaks to our heart. Immediately we understand that the Christian, the child of God will have some bad times, but he can hope in God because God is absolutely rock-like in His faithfulness and love. He will never desert the child of God. There is embodied in the Psalms the experience of men of God who knew the Lord, and out of their experience they wrote what we call "psalms." They are really just hymns of the church under the Old Covenant.

Let's take another example of how God reveals Himself through history and experience, and that is Job. Whether you believe that Job really existed or not, I do; but the whole point is this: Here we have not only the history of a man, but the experience of a man who went through depths of anguish. The whole thing, which is a sizeable portion of the Old Testament, is a revelation of God in the end. There are times when you tremble as you begin to understand the book of Job because you wonder why God could allow so much, but you understand further on in the Bible when you get this little word in the book of James 5:11 "Consider the end of Job." There is the experience of a man, and through it God has revealed Himself. So we have direct speech, direct word, prophecy, and we have history and experience both corporate and personal.

Revelation Through Types and Figures

Then we have types and figures. God has revealed Himself in the Bible through what we call typology or figure. This is one of the things He uses more than anything. All these things, by the way, do overlap; I am only defining them for the sake of convenience. For instance, Noah is a type and the apostle Peter takes up Noah in his letters and tells us that here is a picture of being saved. The ark is a type of the church, and Noah is a type of Christ. You get these kind of types all the way through Scripture.

Jonah is a type. Jesus told us that the only sign that would be given to an evil and adulterous generation was the sign of Jonah who was three days in the belly of the sea monster. The Lord Jesus told us that was a sign of Himself (see Matthew 12:39–40). I do not know if Jonah knew when he was in the fishes' stomach whether, in fact, he was making Scripture or if he had any idea he was a type. I do not think he thought that for one moment. The whole point is that God was revealing Himself, even perhaps unknown to the prophet, through the experience of the prophet. It was not just experience; it was not just history; the man was becoming a type.

The tabernacle is a type of the church, and we are told quite clearly in Hebrews that it is a pattern of the heavenly thing. So it is a wonderful, marvelous type of Christ and His body in which every detail is described; but you cannot push it too far. That is one thing you can say about the tabernacle; you cannot push it too far. Every single point in the tabernacle has symbolic meaning and it is consistent to itself throughout. It is the most glorious example of a type or figure in Scripture.

Another example is in the book of Exodus, the little pool of Marah. The children of Israel had been journeying for some time in the wilderness and they came to a pool. They saw water, they tried to drink it but it was bitter; so it was called *Marah*, which means "bitterness." They were very discomforted and very unhappy about the brackish water, and they all groaned and moaned at Moses and Aaron. Moses asked the Lord and He told him to cut down a tree by the side of the pool and cast it into the waters, and the waters became sweet. What is all that about? I know, of course, that some have said that the wood was a certain kind of wood and a few other things, trying to explain it away by saying it was all very scientific. However, the real point of the matter is that here we have a type of lives which are as bitter and brackish as can be until the cross is brought into them. It is by the cross that there is sweetness, and life-giving qualities are produced, and it becomes refreshing and cooling and life-giving again. It is a type.

Again, take the dove. Here is a classic example of a type because throughout Scripture from beginning to end the symbol of the dove is always the same. It speaks always of the Holy Spirit from the beginning to the end. Not only that, you will find that in every connection of the dove it is always to do with the new nature; it is always to do with heaven. I am not going to explain it but just to mention it. It is very interesting that the raven is always in connection with the other side.

Another symbol, which is just as interesting is the serpent as we have already mentioned. From the beginning of the Bible right through to the last book of the Bible, the serpent is always a symbol of evil, a symbol of Satan, that great adversary of God.

Revelation in Theophany

There is another way in which God has revealed Himself in the Bible, and it is what we call theophany or the actual visitation of God to this earth. There are a number of examples, and I will give you one definite example and mention a few possibilities. Read Exodus 19, the whole passage, down to the end of that chapter. There, Moses gazed upon God. It was a theophany. God actually revealed Himself before Moses and before the people. The people only saw the thunders and the lightning and the cloud upon Mount Sinai, but Moses went up and met God and saw Him. So tremendous was the vision of God that he had to put a veil over his face because people could not look upon him (see Exodus 34:33–35). That is only one of what we call theophanies of the Old Testament. There are many others and some of them are fascinating.

For instance, who was it that went and stayed with Abraham and had a meal with him with two others? It seems at first that they are three angels, but you will remember that Sarah was behind the tent flap listening to the conversation. Of course, she should not have been there, but there she was with her ear glued behind the tent flap listening to the conversation. She heard the angel or one of the angels who was evidently in charge of the other two say to Abraham, "At the right time of the year your wife will bear a child." Sarah, of course, was about ninety-eight and she gave a quiet or perhaps not so quiet cackle behind the door flap of the tent. The story goes that not the angel but the Lord said to Sarah, "Why did you laugh?" And Sarah immediately said through the tent flap, "I did not laugh." It is very interesting that "the Lord said." Was that a theophany?

Who is Melchizedek? Is he just used as a symbol by the writer of the Hebrews when he said, "Who had neither beginning nor end, had neither father nor mother"? There are those, of course, who believe that Melchizedek was a theophany. There are others of us who do not. We believe that Melchizedek was a man used as a symbol.

Then again, who was the one who met Joshua outside the walls of Jericho and said, "I am the Captain of the Lord's hosts"? He bade Joshua to take his shoes from off his feet, and Joshua worshiped

Him. By the way, no angels in Scripture have ever allowed anyone to worship them. Who was He?

Who was the angel of the Lord who wrestled with Jacob at the ford of Jabbok and who Jacob besought to tell him His name? It is an interesting fact in Scripture that angels normally give their name. They tell you: "I am Gabriel," or "I am Michael." They often give their names as recorded in the Word. However, this one would not tell Jacob His name, but Jacob later described it as the "face of God." He had seen God.

These are just a few possibilities. There are other actual visitations of God, but these are the mysteries that we have in the Old Testament where God, as it were, revealed Himself, expressed Himself in one way or another. Of course we get this term the angel of the Lord, and it is very easy just to say that the angel of the Lord is a mere angel until you investigate the term, and then you come up against something which is very, very difficult indeed to describe. He is either the Lord Himself or you have no other explanation. Again I will leave that matter.

Jesus is the Supreme Revelation of God

So we have all these different ways—direct speech, prophecy, history and experience, types and figures, and theophany. But the supreme way that God has revealed Himself in the Bible is of course through the Lord Jesus Christ Himself. He is the supreme and full revelation of God. We read in John 1:14: these wonderful words: "And the Word became flesh, and dwelt among us and we beheld his glory, glory as of the only begotten from the Father, full of grace and truth."

Verses 16–18: "For of his fullness we all received, and grace for grace. For the law was given through Moses; grace and truth came through Jesus Christ. No man hath seen God at any time; the only begotten Son, who is in the bosom of the Father, he hath declared him." He has brought Him into full view; He has manifested Him.

It is the Lord Jesus who is the summit of revelation in the Bible. It is as if the Son comes out in full splendour. It is yet a progressive revelation. It is rather like the sunrise in the mountains. When the sun first begins to rise, you just see here and there a few peaks that are caught in the rays of the rising sun. But as the sun really begins to soar in the heavens, every shadow is dispersed and you begin to see everything as it really is; everything is bathed in sunshine. So it is with God's Word. It is as if at the very beginning you see just a few peaks here and there that are caught in the rays of God's light, of His revelation, and then as the sun rises we see more and more and more clearly.

The Body of Christ

Again, I think we ought to say that it is not only the Lord Jesus Himself who is the supreme and full revelation of God, but there is one other way in which God has revealed Himself in the Bible and that is through the body of Christ, His church. We must remember that the New Testament has been given to us through the Holy Spirit by the early church. This revelation is completed by the Holy Spirit through members of the body of Christ. So we have all the letters of the apostles and others, we have the Gospels that record the actual ministry and life of Christ, and we have the Acts, which records the history, the first years of the church.

This revelation is a unity. We need all the parts to fully understand the whole and we need the whole to fully understand the parts. It is very important that we understand that. We need all the parts to understand the whole and we need the whole to understand fully all the parts. Each throws light on the other. No one piece of Scripture can be isolated and privately interpreted.

Scripture Interprets Scripture

II Peter 1:20 is a verse which has given quite a lot of trouble in its translation because it could mean a number of things. This is the way the Revised Standard Version has translated it. "First of all, you must understand this, that no prophecy of scripture is a matter of one's own interpretation." The Standard Version put it in a slightly different way: "No scripture is of private interpretation." Darby puts it: "no prophecy explains itself." No scripture can stand on its own.

Whatever we might understand by the various translations, one thing is clear: You cannot isolate any Scripture or any text or any part of the Word, any parable, any story or any experience and build on it some great or important doctrine. You cannot do that. All Scripture holds together; it has to be compared and understood in the light of the whole. It is dangerous to build a big doctrine on an isolated verse or a story or parable. We ought to just say that because it will preserve us from an awful lot of trouble if we will always understand that Scripture interprets Scripture, it is a progressive revelation, and that every part of it must be seen within the compass of the whole.

I think we ought to say that in this revelation not every part is as important. Now be careful in the way you understand what I say. I once said this and some people deduced from what I said that some parts of God's Word were not very necessary and therefore did not need to be heeded. I think we have to understand that this revelation, although it is tremendous and every part of it is important, not every part is as important or as final or as profound. For instance, no one is going to tell me that a whole chapter of genealogies is as profound as a chapter in the Song of Songs. Of course, I am glad that we have the genealogical tables. It is good that we have them; they are important and necessary to the whole revelation, but they are not as profound as, for instance, Isaiah 53 or the 22nd Psalm. Are you going to tell me that some other part of the Scriptures is as profound as that? Although this revelation is tremendous and every part of it is necessary, not every part is as important or as final as some other parts. Of course, to neglect or ignore any part of this Book is to harm oneself spiritually, and that needs to be said. It is amazing the way people can be helped from a part of God's Word in which others might wonder if there was any real value there. Yet it is a strange thing that sometimes it is just those parts which God uses to speak to a person when in real need.

Revelation is a Principle

We must also say that if the Bible is an unveiling of God beyond our natural ability to attain to or properly understand, it follows that we cannot approach it in an ordinary way. We cannot approach it as we would approach Shakespeare or Goethe or Tolstoy. What can I say? I could mention Pasternak or one or two today that some people would consider, and I consider it in some way to be the work of genius, but you cannot just approach the Bible as you would approach those works. You just cannot do it because they are not an unveiling of God. The Bible claims to be *the* unveiling of God, authoritative and unique; therefore, it has to be approached on an altogether different level to any other literature.

Revelation is a principle. It is true that the created can never fully understand the Creator. The thing which is created does not have the capacity to fully comprehend the One who has created it. If you and I are to understand God then it has to be revealed to us. He has got to reveal Himself to us, and the Bible is the revelation of God. But we must have the eyes of our heart enlightened, for it is not enough to have the revelation.

Some people seem to think this: "The Bible is a revelation of God, so that is all we need then. Therefore, all we have to do is read the Bible and begin to study it. We will begin to compare different things and really see if we can get hold of what this Book is about." Right, it is the revelation of God; it is the unveiling of God. If it is the unveiling of God and God has given it to us, let us get on with the job.

However, that is the whole point. It is not only that God has revealed Himself in this Book, but also before you and I can understand that revelation we have to have the eyes of our heart enlightened. Can I put it this way? A person without sight can be in a room flooded with light showing the most beautiful and the most expensive and valuable things; yet they cannot see them.

I was at a conference for the blind some years ago and I shared a room with a dear Christian brother who was completely blind. He was injured in the war and he had no eyeballs at all. I had no experience before of being with blind people, so the first shock I got was when we were outside. It was such a lovely warm day, and I thought he would know it was a beautiful day. But I found, of course, that he was in permanent darkness. He did not even know that the sun was up. The only way he could tell was sometimes by the heat. But if it was cold and the wind was blowing, he did not know that the sun was shining. I had always thought that being blind was rather like shutting your eyes and seeing a kind of reddish light somewhere. When I was going to bed, I said to him, "What should I do about the light?" He just simply said to me, "Oh, do not worry about the light; you can leave it on all night. I do not know whether it is on or off." So I said, "I am awfully sorry." He said, "Go, cut it off." Well, I did not feel that I could cut it off. He could have fallen or something happen to him if I cut it off. You cannot live his experience. But the thing that brought it home to me was that the only way he could tell whether a light was on or not in the room was in knowing where the lamp sits. He could go over to it and put his hand on it. If he got burned, he knew it was on. It was the only way he could tell that there was light in the room. That room was flooded with light, and I could see everything; but he could not because he was in blackness.

The Bible is just like that. It is flooded with God's light, but if you do not have spiritual sight you cannot see it. All you can do is use your own intellectual ability or your own natural intelligence, and there is a sense in which you can become more confused and more bewildered than ever. That is why the Scripture speaks about being given sight, about having the eyes of our heart enlightened. In other words, for you to be able to see, you have to have an organ in your head which is able to take the light and make sense of it. Therefore, there are two sides to Christian revelation. God has revealed Himself in what we call the Bible; that is the revelation of God. The other side is that before you and I can understand, we have to be given spiritual sight.

Ephesians 1:17–18a: "That the God of our Lord Jesus Christ, the Father of glory, may give unto you a spirit of wisdom and revelation in the knowledge of him; having the eyes of your heart enlightened, that ye may know ..."

Matthew 16:17: "And Jesus answered and said unto him, Blessed art thou, Simon Bar-Jonah: for flesh and blood hath not revealed it unto thee, but my Father who is in heaven."

The Natural Man's Understanding

1 Corinthians 2:6–16 makes is quite clear that the natural man does not receive the things of God for they are foolishness unto him. His way of reckoning, his scale of values make him understand these things as folly. They are just silly; they are irrational; they are illogical; they do not make sense. He does not have the capacity. It is very much like my preparing a beautiful garden for someone who is blind. I decide to put some colours there and other colours here. I will put the tall things behind and I will put the smaller things in front, and it will be a blaze of colour. I think my friend will be absolutely enraptured by it, but when my friend comes, he cannot see a thing. Not only does my friend say he cannot see a thing, but furthermore he tells me that I am mad. "There is no such thing as that flower there and another one here; it does not make sense," he tells me. I try to explain to him the different kinds of plants, but he tells me that he is not even sure such things exist. What can I do? He does not have the faculty of sight, so he can only

go by my experience. Therefore, he naturally feels that I am to be treated with great suspicion.

The point is that self-sufficient knowledge is in great danger of stumbling, stemming as it does from the fall. When man first ate of the tree of the knowledge of good and evil, he took something into himself which made him a self-sufficient type of person. His self-sufficiency grew out of his own capacity for knowledge, for being able to store knowledge and to be able to decide what is what. When this self-sufficient type of knowledge tries to get into the things of God, you straightaway have trouble. The natural man receiveth not the things of God—the natural man, whether Christian or non-Christian. He may be a child of God, but he may still be trying to use the old natural man in the things of God, using the wrong vehicle. You are getting yourself into trouble because of that. Upon that type of mentality and that type of approach there rests a divine veto.

God has given us a revelation of Himself. He has unveiled His character. He has unveiled His purpose. He has unveiled His salvation, and it is all found within the covers of this volume we call the Bible, God's Word.

The Meaning of Inspiration

Now I will share something about inspiration. It is a twin subject to revelation. What do we mean by inspiration? The *Oxford Dictionary* gives the meaning as: "to breathe in, to inhale, to infuse thought or feeling into someone." However, this is not the scriptural idea of inspiration at all, and we must make the difference very, very clear to begin with. The Biblical idea of inspiration is not someone infusing some thoughts or feelings into certain men who then wrote them down.

The word used in II Timothy 3:16 is this: "Every scripture inspired of God is also profitable for teaching, for reproof, for correction, for instruction which is in righteousness." The alternative, which is in the margin of the Revised Standard and Authorized Version, is rendered "all Scripture is inspired of God." Now the word we want is: *inspired of God*. What does this mean? The Greek word we have translated *inspired* means literally "God breathed," and it actually means "breathed out" rather than "breathed in." It is in fact important that we should understand the difference. The Bible is not the result of God inspiring certain men with certain thoughts, to use the *Oxford Dictionary* definition, sort of infusing thoughts and feelings into certain prophets and other men of God, playing on their artistic or spiritual capabilities, where after they then wrote down something which we now call the Scriptures. The Bible is the result of God the Spirit within those men *breathing out* the Word of God. Now it may not seem at first sight to be a very great difference, but it is in fact fundamental. The Scripture teaches us that it was God the Holy Spirit in those men who breathed out the Word of God.

We have looked at II Timothy 3:16, now let us see whether that is so as we read I Peter 1:10–11. I want you to note this very carefully because the Scriptural doctrine of inspiration is very interesting and is so often misunderstood. "Concerning which salvation the prophets sought and searched diligently, who prophesied of the grace that should come unto you: searching what time or what manner of time the Spirit of Christ which was *in* them did point unto, when it testified beforehand the sufferings of Christ, and the glories that should follow them."

It does not say "the Spirit of Christ which was on them." That is the general idea of inspiration. The Spirit of God was on those men, influencing them, putting ideas into them. The scriptural doctrine of inspiration is that the Holy Spirit was *in* them and speaking from *within* to without.

II Peter 1:19–21: "And we have the word of prophecy made more sure; whereunto ye do well that ye take heed, as unto a lamp shining in a dark place, until the day dawn, and the day-star arise in your hearts: knowing this first, that no prophecy of scripture is of private interpretation. For no prophecy ever came by the will of man" The Revised Standard Version puts "by the impulse of man." It is a rather interesting word—"by the impulse of man, by the will of man."

"No Scripture or prophecy ever came by the will of man, but men spake from God." It is not men spake of God, but they spoke *from* God. God was doing this thing and they were a kind of vessel "being moved by the Holy Spirit." The word is: *being borne along.* They were being carried by the Holy Spirit.

Hebrews 1:1–2a: "God, having of old time spoken unto the fathers in the prophets (not through the prophets, but in the prophets) by divers portions and in divers manners, hath at the end of these days spoken unto us in his Son." It was in the prophets that God spoke. Therefore, when we speak of divine inspiration of the Bible, we do not mean that it is inspiring or inspirable.

We once had a dear lady, a theatrical lady, who was very interested in things as a result of a Billy Graham campaign. I remember once she sat in the hall talking away and someone mentioned something about divine inspiration of the Bible. She said, "Oh yes, of course it is. I find it divinely inspiring." Of course, that is not divine inspiration of the Bible. It is not just divinely inspiring, although that puts into a nutshell the thought of a lot of moderns. Just because it inspires you, that part of it is inspired. That is not the biblical doctrine of inspiration. It is not inspiring or inspirable, though of course it is both, but that is not what it means here.

Nor does it mean that God is breathing through the Scriptures. That is another modern idea: God is just sort of breathing through the Scriptures. Of course, that is true, but it is not the biblical doctrine of inspiration. Nor is it that the Scriptures breathe out God. Biblical inspiration is that God has breathed out Scripture. It is as simple as that. The Bible has been produced by God through the Holy Spirit in certain men. It is, therefore, in a different class altogether to the inspired work of human genius. That has come by another form of inspiration. I am not for one moment saying that God cannot inspire certain things. It may well be that certain human works have been inspired by God, that is, there has been a divine impression made upon a life. Using again the *Oxford Dictionary* definition: certain thoughts or feelings have been infused, and as a result certain works have resulted. I am not only thinking of religious works, but what are sometimes called secular works. It may be that some can be called inspired in that sense, but the Bible is not the result of that kind of inspiration at all. The Bible is the result of God Himself, in certain men, by the Holy Spirit breathing out what we call the Scriptures.

Inspiration and the Bible's Construction

I want you also to note that this inspiration covers every part and phase in the construction of God's Word, the Bible—every part. God was in the prophets, in their human temperament and background. It does not matter whether it was Jeremiah, who was a very dramatic person, one day up in the heavens, the next day down in the trough of deepest despair, God was in him; or whether it was Isaiah, with his great cultured background, his royal blue blood. God was in him. Whether it was Amos, the shepherd, a man who was not used to culture or high standard at all, God was in him. It might have been Elijah or it may have been Malachi. It could be Moses or Daniel; God was in them. They were different men, with different backgrounds, different temperaments, living at different times, but God was in them. That is one point.

Then again, this word *inspiration* covers the prevailing conditions and knowledge of the day. This causes a lot of trouble with some people. They want to know how much certain of these men, who were used by God in this way, were conditioned by the prevailing knowledge and understanding of their day. Nevertheless, the whole point is that in the last analysis it was the Almighty God who was in them, who knows all things, who in fact spoke.

Later, we will deal with the relationship of the divine and the human in this question of inspiration, or try to deal with it because it is almost an undealable subject. What I am saying is that this word inspiration covers every single phase and part of the construction of the Bible. So it does not matter whether it is right back in antiquity in Ur of the Chaldees, or whether it is in Babylon or Nineveh or

Rome or Jerusalem; it is God the Holy Spirit in these men who is breathing out His Word.

I want you to notice something else which I think is often overlooked. The word used for "every Scripture inspired of God," is not every *saying* inspired of God but every *scripture*. The word used means "the written thought." So this word *inspiration* covers not merely what was orally given but what was transmitted into writing. It was not only that which was given at the time by preaching or by word, but the way it was finally put down into written form as we have it. The word is Scripture. So again this word *inspiration* covers every part and phase of the construction of God's Word.

The Scriptural idea of inspiration does not, however, mean a mechanical dictation or the putting aside of human personality and will. In this it differs from the Gentile idea of inspiration common in the days when the Bible was actually being compiled and still common today in Spiritism and other things. The idea of inspiration there is of possession in which the human will and personality is entirely suspended and something else within talks and speaks and reveals, even gives dictation. But this is not the inspiration of God's Word. In no place in God's Word does inspiration mean the suspension of human will or personality. It is very much the opposite, in actual fact. Of course, there may be ecstasy with revelation and we English people on the whole are rather afraid of ecstasy, but it is true that there is such a thing as ecstasy. Sometimes it does go with revelation, but for those of you who want to look up this matter you will find a very interesting little aside in I Corinthians 14. Concerning this very matter of revelation, and tongues and all the ecstatic things in an atmosphere of ecstasy, it says, "And the spirits of the prophets are subject to the prophets" (v. 32). In other words, the Biblical idea of inspiration never means the loss of self-control. That is very important to understand.

This revelation of God, in a way which is itself impressive, has been given by the Holy Spirit in and through men at different times and of different temperaments, in the style, the methods and the vocabulary of their own day. If the Lord wills we will look at those differences and compare certain men (their backgrounds) with each other and see the other side of the picture.

The Living Word and the Written Word

One of the great Bible scholars of the past generation pointed out that there was a most remarkable similarity between the living Word and the written Word, in the sense that the living Word, being Christ, is both God and man. It is almost impossible for us to distinguish what is man and what is God. The two have mingled together in a mystery. It is also true about the written Word; we are up against a mystery. We have on the one side the divine and on the other side we have the human, and the two mingle. Try as we can to distinguish them, it is sometimes very hard. At the same time it is perhaps a most instructive and corrective thing to actually investigate these matters because you can either have an idea of inspiration which rules out human personality and will altogether, making people little automatons who just simply say something that is coming from within them; or you can go to the other extreme and say that it is all human activity with God standing, as it were, in the wings sort of giving a little bit of encouragement and generally influencing things to go in the right direction. Neither of those two views are right. It is in some amazing union between God and man that you really have the heart of the matter.

3.
The Inspiration of the Bible

We are going to take up this matter of divine inspiration again. I want very simply to remind you of what we said about inspiration. You will remember that the *Oxford Dictionary* says that the meaning of *inspiration* or to *inspire* is firstly "to inhale, breathe in, infuse thoughts or feelings into another." This is not at all the biblical idea of inspiration. When God's Word uses the word *inspire*, it has an altogether different meaning. It does not mean that God is playing on the artistic or literary or so-called spiritual abilities of certain men, giving them ideas or influencing them perhaps to write certain things or say certain things. The idea is a compound word as in II Timothy 3:16: "Every scripture inspired of God ..." is "every scripture God inspired," and the idea is more of something breathed out rather than breathed in.

The Spoken and Written Word

We looked at a number of scriptures and underlined the little preposition *in*; "God hath spoken aforetime to the fathers *in* the prophets" (see Hebrews 1:1). Again, "... the Spirit of Christ which was in them did point unto, when it predicted the sufferings of Christ and the subsequent glory" (see I Peter 1:11). We also looked at the other scripture that speaks of men of God being borne along, being moved by the Holy Spirit. The idea all through of divine inspiration is that God, by the Holy Spirit, was *within* these men and was actually giving expression *within* them to His own heart and mind. He was breathing out Scripture through them.

We also noticed that this term inspiration covers not just the spoken or preached Word, but also the written Word. For it is the most interesting thing that in II Timothy 3:14–16 the word that is used is "sacred writings." Then he says, "all Scripture inspired of God," not just every word of God inspired of Him or not just every saying, but every Scripture, which is the actual written Word. The word used is a technical word for the written Word. It not only covers the oral transmission of God's Word, but also the written form of God's Word.

Therefore, this word *inspiration* covers every stage in the construction of the Bible, from its actually being given, as it were, orally in some cases, right down to its being transmitted into its written form. God was in those who spoke and wrote. That is very important. Therefore, we can say straightaway that the Bible has been produced by God through the Holy Spirit in certain men.

The biblical idea of inspiration is not one of mechanical dictation. God did not, more or less dictate what He had to say to a kind of human vessel like an automatic machine that followed word for word. The Gentile view of inspiration, common in the days of the Lord Jesus and indeed all the way through, the compilation of Scripture, was of possession by a spirit with the complete suspension of human will and thought. In other words, you still see it today in Spiritism and in some of the other religions of the world where there is a view and an experience of inspiration that is not divine. It is the complete suspension of the human mind and human will so that a person becomes, as it were, just a machine through which something else writes or speaks. This is not at all the biblical idea of inspiration.

The Divine and Human Aspect of the Scriptures

This revelation of God, which we call the Bible, in a way which is itself impressive, has been given by the Holy Spirit in and through different men at different times in the style and method and vocabulary of their own day. It is, however, this mysterious connection between the divine and human aspects of the Scriptures which is both baffling and instructive. That is the matter we are going to deal with now. In one way it is fascinating and most instructive, but I must say at the beginning, that by the time we finish you ought to be instructed in certain things and highly baffled in others. When you really seek to analyze this whole matter of the human and the divine aspect of God's Word—where they fuse, how they mingle together and how they are connected—you are touching something which is a first class mystery. It is impossible to get to the root of it except to draw certain deductions, which we will seek to do.

Men Moved by the Holy Spirit

What does the Bible really mean by inspiration? We understood that it means God was inside those men, within them and He was breathing out His heart and His mind. He was producing, creating His Word in them and through them; but how much of it was influenced by man? What part of the transmission of God's Word was man's? Can we draw it in a line? Second Peter 1:21 sums up the whole thing: "No prophecy ever came by the impulse of man," or the Authorised Version, "the will of man." "For no prophecy ever came by the impulse of man: but men, moved by the Holy Spirit spoke from God." Here we have the mystery. On the one side, nothing ever came by the impulse of man. If you just took that, then man was out of it. But on the other hand, it is "but men ..." There is an emphasis in the Word on the word *men*, and it is rightly emphasized. Men spoke; not that the Holy Spirit spoke through men, but men spoke by the Holy Spirit: "... men moved by the Holy Spirit spoke from God."

This whole verse is most interesting and most instructive because this little word *moved* is the same word that you will find in Acts 27:15, 17. It can be translated "borne along" and in fact it is used here in Acts 27:15 in another connection, but it is interesting to see it. "And when the ship was caught, and could not face the wind, we gave way to it, and were driven" (verse 15). It is the same word, were borne along.

"And when they had hoisted it up, they used helps, under-girding the ship; and, fearing lest they should be cast upon the Syrtis, they lowered the gear, and so were driven" (verse 17).

Again, it is interesting that this same word is used of the Holy Spirit in another connection in Acts 2:2: "And suddenly there came from heaven a sound as of the rushing of a mighty wind." The word *rushing* is the exact same word. The idea is of something "borne along."

Now this scripture speaks of men, "no prophecy ever came by impulse of man or will of man but men borne along by the Holy Spirit spake from God." Again, it is interesting that in the New English Bible it has been put like this in II Peter 1:20, 21: "For it was not through any human whim that men prophesied of old. Men they were, but impelled by the Holy Spirit they spoke the words of God." The thought there is caught—"impelled." Immediately you have on the one hand that it was not the impulse of man; on the other hand, you get human agency in its own right and yet you get the direction and control of the Holy Spirit. What is the end? Words spoken from God. They are not words spoken *of* God, nor words spoken *about* God but words spoken *from* God. God was there and He was speaking, and these men became, as it were, a mouthpiece of God.

Divine Compulsion

When you understand just a little bit of this, it brings you to this problem of what I call "divine compulsion." This divine compulsion, in the actual producing of God's Word, was neither physical nor psychological. It certainly did not involve the setting aside of the personality or the character or the will of the human vessel. Indeed, it would seem that this divine direction and compulsion used the originality of the human vessel to the full in the most remarkable ways. Breathing through their particular personality and character quite naturally, the whole impression was rightly one of complete naturalness, spontaneity, and freedom. There was the impelling force, direction, and control of the Holy Spirit, yet there was a complete and willing cooperation, perhaps at times unconscious, between the human side and the divine side. Now this is the mystery, and how to get beyond that I do not know. We shall look at some of the symptoms, if you like, of the whole matter of this subject, but whether we shall get any further I am not sure.

One of the things that is the most remarkable and most baffling factor in Scripture is its obvious spontaneity and freedom in its writing. It does seem as if the human authors, the human writers were completely spontaneous and completely free. Take for instance, the apostle Paul, and some of the asides he makes. We have to ask ourselves, if this is by inspiration of God here is spontaneity and freedom which is quite remarkable and something altogether removed from our idea of what inspiration entails. We would not, for instance, expect Paul to say some of the things he says about himself or some of the statements he makes now and again, not in the main way but in a sort of aside. On the one hand, you have the Holy Spirit within these men impelling them so that they speak from God. On the other hand, their originality, their spontaneity, their freedom of expression does not seem to be in any way limited or restricted. I think we must underline that. The outcome of all of this was God-inspired Scripture.

Note Mark 12:36, and this is the Lord Jesus talking: "David himself said in the Holy Spirit ..." Again, you have the two sides, but the emphasis is on David's words. "David said ..." Yet we are told that David spoke in the Holy Spirit. David was enveloped by the Holy Spirit, and he was, as it were, encircled by the Holy Spirit. Not only was the Holy Spirit within David, but David was within the Holy Spirit when he spoke. The Lord Jesus was emphasising the human aspect. It was David who spoke, but it was the Holy Spirit who evidently was the source. Here again is the mystery of the human and divine aspect of God's Word. Keep in mind that the Lord Jesus was quoting Psalm 110, and here He says, "David spake in the Holy Spirit."

In Hebrews 1:13 it says: "But of which of the angels hath he" (God) "said at any time, Sit thou on my right hand, till I make thine enemies the footstool of thy feet?" There is no mention of David saying anything. It is purely and simply, "God hath said." Jesus said, "David said in the Holy Spirit." The writer of Hebrews says, "God hath said."

Again, Acts 1:16 and this is from another Psalm of David: "Brethren," said Peter, "it was needful that the scripture should be fulfilled, which the Holy Spirit spake before by the mouth of David ..." This is the Holy Spirit speaking by the mouth of David concerning Judas.

Acts 2:25: "For David saith concerning him ..." Now it is only the human authorship. Nothing is even mentioned of God or the Holy Spirit having anything to do with it.

Verse 34: "For David ascended not into the heavens: but he said himself ..." Again, it is David.

We have to take into consideration a large number of phrases such as these, and these are all scriptural phrases that I am going to quote.

"Moses saith," "Moses wrote," "Isaiah saith," "Isaiah crieth," "Isaiah did prophesy," "the Scripture saith," "It saith." All of these are phrases describing parts of God's Word. It does not mean that there are various degrees and differing measures of inspiration as some have tried to point out. They feel that where it says, "David spake in the Holy Spirit," there is a high degree of inspiration, a high inspirational content, and where it says, "God said," that is the highest inspirational content. But when you come down to something else, it may just be the human vessel inspired, but just a human vessel. I do not think this at all because if you study carefully all these Scriptures, especially where the same quotation is quoted more than once, you will come to this conclusion that all these phrases are equated with the simple one, "God saith." In other words, you are again up against this simple mystery of the divine and the human aspect of God's Word, so simple that the Scriptures themselves speak of it in quite a simple way. "Moses saith here," and another place it will say, "The Lord spoke through the prophet saying ..." Or again it will say, "It saith so and so." Or another time it will just use the phrase, "The Scripture saith ..." In other places it speaks of "God saith."

A Full View of the Lord Jesus

Again, it is instructive to note that when God wishes to give us a full-orbed view of His Son, He takes four different men who say the same thing in four different ways—Matthew, Mark, Luke, and John. Now, if inspiration were a mechanical thing or just a question of a mechanical dictation, if God could so use a human vessel as to make it just like a human typewriter, then we would not need four different men. We would need only one, and by having one writer we would iron out a whole number of difficulties that we find in the four Gospels. Here you are again in the presence of a mystery because for a full-orbed view of Christ, God uses four different men. He takes Matthew who is obviously by nature more of a traditionalist. When you read the Gospel of Matthew carefully, you will find that his whole feelings, his whole personality is steeped in the past. The thing that thrills him about Christ is that He is the Messianic King who has utterly fulfilled all the desires of Israel and all the prophecies concerning the Messianic kingdom which was to come.

The Gospel of Mark was probably written very much under the influence of Peter. We find in Mark a different personality altogether, someone who is much more simple and who somehow or other ties everything down to the servant. The theme of Mark is "Christ as the Servant," and he sees Christ as the Servant of the Lord serving everyone, the One who came not only to serve God but to serve the world, and to serve His own. There was no better person probably than either Mark or Peter, no one more fitted to speak of Christ in this way.

Then you have Dr. Luke, the third Gospel, and Luke's whole approach is different. He is most interested, for instance, in diseases. In the Gospel of Luke you have a more detailed analysis of the people who are ill than in any other Gospel, as you would expect. Luke is a physician and being a physician, he is interested in men and women as physical men and women, and so his whole Gospel sees Christ as a Man. The thing that thrills the writer of Luke's Gospel is the fact that Christ is the Son of Man and it is a revelation of Christ as human, touched with the feeling of the people.

When you come to John, you soar away into the heavens. John's whole revelation of Christ is not as King merely, not as Servant, not as Man; His revelation of Jesus is as the Word, the living Word, who has neither beginning nor end—God the Son. John was no traditionalist. Right the way through his Gospel he is comparing the old dispensation with what Christ has brought in. He chooses eight different miracles to prove the fact that Christ has finished and closed the old dispensation and opened a new age. Matthew does not tell us that. It is not that Matthew clashes with John; it is rather that the Holy Spirit in Matthew has given us another aspect of Christ. Now you have four Gospels, divinely inspired, God-breathed-out, and yet there are four different men that have been chosen to be the vessels of this many-sided, full-orbed view of the fullness of Christ.

Different Aspects of Doctrine in the Bible

It is virtually the same with the letters, in which we find the same thing. God takes a Paul when He wants to speak about justification through faith. I do believe Paul was absolutely qualified in God's preparation of him, right from his birth, to be able in the end to speak of justification through faith. No man ever lived more purely by the law; no man ever saw more into the meaning of the law; he was trained in the law. However, when the day came that God met him on the Damascus road and revealed His Son in him, something happened in Paul which broke the old law, and he became the apostle of faith. Now if God wants to speak to us about justification through faith, the end of an old order, the death of the law, then he takes a man like Paul. There was no man more free than Paul. You can see it. His words run away with him. He is the kind of man who is by nature free.

Then, when God wants to speak to us about works, he takes a man like James. There is no funny business with James. James is almost acid; he is intensely practical. He has no time at all for this talk of justification through faith unless it is proved by works. He preaches the same doctrine (and has given many a headache over it) with a completely different angle, but he calls it works. However, when you investigate and study it closely, you find it is the same doctrine with a different garb, that's all. God takes a James, a man who by nature is more legal in some aspects, and through him He reveals this whole matter of good works and their necessity.

If God wants to speak to us about eternal security, who does he take? He takes John, the apostle who speaks of eternal security. He is the only one who has recorded for us those words: "No man, no one can pluck them out of My Father's hand. I know My sheep and in the last day I will raise them up." Word after word after word comes out of John. All through his Gospel it is about the eternal security of the redeemed and how they will never be lost. John tells us that if they went out from us, they were not of us; that is the explanation. He did not believe it was anything about losing your salvation. Nothing like that with John. He said, "If they go out and never come back, it is a sign that they were never really born of God," because his attitude in his Letters is: "Whatsoever is born of God overcometh the world." He is absolutely definite about it. There is no question of it. If there is just a little something born of God in you, it will overcome in the end. It will be there in the glory. That is John's attitude.

However, when the Lord wants to warn us about the awful possibility of losing our inheritance and receiving eternal harm and injury, he takes another person. We do not even know who it is, but it is the writer to the Hebrews. Through him he starts to warn us from beginning to end that if we neglect so great a salvation, what will happen to us? If we draw back to perdition ... if, if, if. His great word is *if,* and he is underlining all the time the possibility of losing an inheritance. All these letters, all these parts of the New Testament are God-breathed-out. That is the divine side, but the human side is a Paul, a James, a writer of the Hebrews, and John.

The Difference of Style within the Bible

I would like you to note the difference that there is in style in the Bible. Evidently, inspiration does not mean sameness of style. This is an idea many of us would have, that if God really was in them they would surely have sameness of style; it would be a divine style. But in fact, there is no such thing. We have a tremendous variety of style.

If you compare Genesis, Daniel, and Song of Solomon, you will see the difference in style. Take any portion of Genesis, any portion of Daniel, any portion of the Song of Solomon, and put them together, the simplest believer would know that they came from different parts of God's Word. There is a difference of style within them. Someone says, "Of course, you will have a difference of style between Genesis and Song of Solomon, there were a lot of centuries between the two."

Let's take then Isaiah and Ezekiel. They are nearer to each other. Look at the difference in style between these two men. Ezekiel's style is a literary style to start with, and he does not have a gift of oratory. I am quite sure if Ezekiel had preached some of his great messages on the cherubim here, two-thirds of the people would be fast asleep. His whole approach is literary; it is to be studied. You need to sit down and read and study. He has a style which is quiet and it is complex.

Isaiah is different in style. He is the greatest preacher, as far as we can tell, in the Old Testament, and his style is one of oratorical beauty. He soars away into the heavens; there is no one like Isaiah. That is why we all love Isaiah because just to read, especially the latter part of the book, is a joy. It is not simply what he says; it is the way he says it. It is a style that you surely would not mix up with anything from Ezekiel. It would be most interesting to pull sections of different things from the Bible, hand them out, and see if you knew where they came from. I wonder if anyone would really mix up Ezekiel with Isaiah? For those of you who have read your Bible just a little bit more, I doubt whether anyone would mix those two men; but they are just two examples. There are many others that we could take.

Coming to the New Testament, John has his own definite style. I am sure if you brought any portion of John's writings to me and any portion of Paul's, I could tell the difference straightaway. John has a definite style inherent within everything he has written. There is a possibility that the only thing that would trip you up is the book of Revelation, but that has a reason. However, everything else that is written by John, his letters and his Gospel, have a style that is inherent within them, and the Pauline style is altogether different. You cannot mix up John and Paul. John has a simplicity of style and language against Paul's super abundance of adjectives and much else. You cannot mix up these two styles.

Let's take James. Is anyone going to be muddled as to what is James, what is John, and what is Paul? Those three styles stand out clearly in the New Testament—John, Paul, and James.

The Difference of Method in the Bible

Then, there is the difference of method in the Bible. Inspiration does not mean that the same method has been adopted, especially on the written side of it. For instance, take the acrostic Psalms. Psalm 37 and Psalm 119 are acrostic psalms. What is an acrostic psalm? It is simply that each letter of the Hebrew alphabet, of which there are twenty-two, is used to commence each sentence. In Psalm 37 every two verses begin with the same letter. All of Psalm 119, even in the English version, is divided up into the twenty-two letters of the Hebrew alphabet, and every single verse in each section begins with the letter of its section. Aleph—every single verse in that section begins with Aleph, Beth with Beth, and so on.

If you were to tell someone that God could inspire such things some people would hardly believe it. They would feel that such an involved method could hardly be an embodiment of divine inspiration. Yet the acrostic psalms are just that, and acrostics are found elsewhere. In the little book of Esther the name of the Lord or the name of God is not mentioned once, and yet it is there four times at each turning point of the story. Each time it comes to a crisis, there in the acrostics is the Lord's name, Jehovah or Yahweh; it is there in the book of Esther. Divine inspiration has used different methods, and some of them are most remarkable.

Take the acrostic Psalm 119, with its involved literary method and put it over against Psalm 18, which is that psalm of David's great cry of triumph. At last he comes to the throne and looks back over his whole life. It is a tremendous cry of triumph and it is absolutely spontaneous. Here you have two kinds of methods— one, which is absolutely spontaneous, and is God-breathed-out, and the other, which is a most involved literary method, and it is still God-breathed-out.

Then, take what we call the Mosaic Psalms. By Mosaic Psalms I do not mean the psalms that Moses wrote, but psalms which are Mosaic in their structure. They are all little pieces pinched from other psalms. Did you know that? There are at least two psalms that are literally pinched from all the other psalms. In Psalm 144 there is not a phrase that is not pinched from the rest of the Psalter. Now would you think that could embody divine inspiration? Yet if you read this psalm, in spite of this involved literary method, it is an amazing psalm. Perhaps that is a comfort for someone who does not know how to praise the Lord on a Sunday morning and has to pinch a few phrases from various quarters by which to do it. Know this that even in God's Word there is such a method. I could tell you also that in certain psalms, a whole half of another psalm has been pinched and there is a repetition almost verbatim. You get that in Obadiah as well, in which nearly the whole book of Obadiah is copied or vice-versa from another portion from one of the other prophets. There you are, and yet, here we have divine inspiration; it is God-breathed-out.

Let's look at some other different methods. Take the book of Job, which is an actual drama, written in the form of an ancient drama. Here God uses the theatre almost to put over a tremendous lesson. I am quite sure many Christians will not like me if I say that God has used anything theatrical, and yet here in God's Word

He has actually used dramatic form in the book of Job. There is a prologue and an epilogue. Then there are different movements right the way through from beginning to end with all the different characters coming on with what they have to say. The whole point is a tremendous instruction in this matter of the mystery of suffering. That is Job, and yet it is God-breathed-out.

Alongside Job, look at the Proverbs. We could not find anything more different from the book of Job than the book of Proverbs. Here you have hundreds and hundreds of short pithy sayings, which if you ever feel depressed, go away and read. I guarantee that within a few moments you will have been lifted up. For there in those pithy sayings you will see all kinds of situations and people embodied. There is nothing like the book of Proverbs to speak to contemporary situations. But here is a book, which belongs to the same class of literature as the book of Job. Job belongs to wisdom literature and so does the book of Proverbs, but they are entirely different in method. One is dramatic in its form and the other contains lots of short pithy sayings which get right to the point. The idea was that the wise men as they were called, "the wise," could teach people by these short pithy sayings, these sort of little, short, terse sentences. They could get to the heart of a problem, and people could repeat them and repeat them until they had learned them. They got right in them, and in that way they were taught in divine wisdom. The book of Proverbs is not something to be avoided, but is something to be studied and read, not once but again and again and again.

In the book of Zechariah you have an entirely different method. We call it apocalyptic. It is something that looks forward to the future and sees the future in symbols. These three different parts of God's Word are entirely different in method, and yet all is God-breathed-out Scripture, divinely inspired.

Take the Song of Songs; is it an allegory? I am convinced myself it is an allegory. I know there are some people who believe it is a little love ditty written by King Solomon about either an Egyptian princess or another shepherd girl that he fell for. But I myself believe it is an allegory, as the rabbis said, "Solomon wrote it when he fell before the Lord and he wrote it by inspiration." I believe it is an allegory, the greatest and most wonderful allegory in the Bible concerning Christ and the church. Yes, maybe it came out of Solomon's experience; that may well be, but it is allegorical in method. There you have another method divinely inspired.

Then there is the book of Exodus. If you put the Song of Songs and the book of Exodus side by side, you have two different methods. The book of Exodus is just narrative. The Song of Songs is allegorical, and yet both are God-breathed-out Scripture.

When we come to the New Testament, we find a difference of method. James is a wonderful example of a certain method which actually was not so much New Testament. It belonged to the period when the Old Testament, as it were, was ending and the New Testament age was beginning. It belongs more to the Lord's kind of ministry in the Sermon on the Mount. James has those little paragraphs, little statements, absolutely to the point, and direct. They get right under your skin and are most uncomfortable to read just because they are so straight and dogmatic and clear. However, there is no real connection. If you read through from beginning to end of James' letter, it is hard to find the real theme. It is true that the point is the practical application of things, but in actual fact he ranges over a vast area of things in that little book. It is a different method altogether for instance, than the letter to the Romans. The letter to the Romans is not really a letter; it is a treatise. It was written, not as some kind of personal letter from Paul to saints in Rome who were in a bit of trouble over the question of faith. Paul sat down and felt that the time had come to put into writing this whole matter of faith, and how it was related to everything. So we have this wonderful, what we call, Roman letter, but it is entirely different to the letter of James.

Of course, when we come to the letter to Philemon, we have another letter altogether. It is a little short letter, and very much like the kind of letter any of us might write. I do not think you would probably write about a slave who had run away, but if someone had arrived home today who had been in the far country and had been saved, it is the kind of letter you and I would write. We would write to the boy's parents or to those who were very interested in him and would say, "Look, in the most marvelous way I have come into contact with so and so. He has come to the Lord, but he is a bit afraid about coming home. I am writing this to let you know it is quite all right. We are quite clear that he is born of God and is a changed person. We know that you will be absolutely full of joy about what has happened to him and how he is." That is Scripture, a little tiny letter, but it is another method. Some people scratch their heads and wonder why the letter to Philemon is in there at all; but it is a different method. So we have the Roman letter, the Epistle of James, and the Philemon letter. All three of them are different entirely in method, in the way they are written, and the very objective of them.

Take another example in the New Testament, the book of Acts and the book of Revelation. There you have a difference of methods. Acts is historical narrative; it is a record. It is not a general history.

It is an actual record of the movement of the Holy Spirit in the early days of the church just before Pentecost, and particularly Pentecost and onwards. But when you come to the book of Revelation, there is an altogether different method. Here is a man who sees a vision. Luke did not see any vision, so how did Luke write the story? Dear old Dr. Luke, I have no doubt at all that he interviewed a lot of people—like some people we know who have written such accounts. He probably scribbled down bits and pieces just like a doctor would. When he heard so and so, he would scribble it all down and put it away. Later on, when he heard something else and wrote it down, he decided to keep it all because it might come in handy one day when the record was written. In the end there came a time when Luke put it together as the book of Acts, but the Holy Spirit was within him, and the result was God-breathed-out Scripture.

The Lord used a different method altogether with John, who was in a mine on Patmos. No doubt he was slaving his life away not knowing that he would be released some years afterwards. He probably thought that he would be there the rest of his days. Suddenly, one day he saw the sea become a sea of glass. Some scholars have thought that it was probably the result of looking at the sea because Patmos was a small island. John may well have looked across the sea a number of times as the sun was setting to the mainland where his home was in Ephesus and where he knew all the churches. Well maybe, maybe not; we do not know. All we know is that one day the Lord spoke to John and he saw a vision, and all the things around him suddenly took on a new shape. He saw right into the future and he saw us—yes, us. He saw us in this day and generation, all down through church history right on to the end. In a sense, I do not even know whether John realised or knew it, but he was summarising all the prophetic literature behind him. It would have taken years and years of study to have brought it all together. He was slaving his life away in a mine. He did not have lots of books or other things around him which he could study and refer to. It was a divinely given revelation of the future of things which must come to pass. He could not, he dare not put it down in black and white. It would mean more than his life was worth. He was a political prisoner, so he used the old apocalyptic method. He used symbol after symbol after symbol after symbol, and all that great system, that cruel system that was around him is symbolised in the book of Revelation. It is a difference of method.

The Difference of Vocabulary in the Bible

Then, there is difference of vocabulary. Divine inspiration does not mean, of course, sameness of vocabulary. I think that is obvious. If we take Genesis 1 and Ephesians 1, many thousands of years separate those two chapters. Nevertheless, here in one volume there is a tremendous difference in vocabulary. Ephesians 1 is dealing with the same idea as the first chapters of Genesis, the beginning, and what happened in the beginning. However, if you take Genesis 1 and John 1 and Ephesians 1, and compare them, you will find a difference of vocabulary. That is understandable because many, many years divide between Genesis and John and Paul.

But when you come to other things, it is even more interesting. For instance, the vocabulary of Jeremiah compared with the vocabulary of Isaiah is different. Or take the vocabulary of Ezekiel and compare it with Isaiah; the men used different vocabulary. It is understandable in a way, but they are talking about the same Lord, with a great difference of vocabulary.

In the New Testament, if you look at John's letters and Paul's letters, you find a difference of vocabulary. I have already mentioned dear old Paul and his great abundance of words. He really did surpass all people in his use of words. They could fall out of him one after another, so much so that sometimes it was not even good Greek. It just simply poured out of him.

It was not so with John. His whole mentality was a more concise one. As Mr. Sparks said, "You find it in his little short sayings in his letters, 'God is love; God is light,'" and so on. Have you ever noticed that Paul does not use that kind of method at all? You never find him saying, "God is love." When Paul talks about God being love he uses at least five adjectives and a lot more. Read in Ephesians what he says about the "exceeding abundance of his love." It is in Ephesians 3 if you think I am exaggerating. It is about the depth, the height, the length, the breath and the exceeding greatness of his love, and so on. That is Paul, but you cannot mix the two men up; their vocabulary is quite different, and yet they were contemporaries. God needed a Paul when he wanted to speak about the eternal mystery hidden from ages and generations but revealed now. He wanted a John when He wanted to soar in simplicity into the heavens and leave us with some of the most profound things about the Lord Jesus that have ever been written. So we can see a little of the difference of vocabulary.

What about the Hebrew letter? What about its vocabulary? Did Paul write it? Many people do not believe that Paul wrote the letter to the Hebrews. They say the vocabulary is quite different, for instance, to the vocabulary in the Roman letter. However, there is a difference of vocabulary even amongst the contemporary writers of the New Testament.

The Difference in Personality in the Bible

Or again, look at the difference in personality. It comes out quite clearly in the Scriptures, and it is clearer in certain parts than in others. But there is a complete, clear difference in personality. This may sound trite, but when you are talking about God-breathed-out Scripture, the mentality of some people is that the human personality has been suspended, and that God is in them having suspended their personality, and their will and much else. It is as if He were speaking through them; it is just God, and they are just a kind of channel, as we sometimes say, "channels only." There is nothing else to it. There is no originality; there is no influence of their character. There is nothing of their personality intruding. It is just God.

But is that so? You only have to look at the Scriptures, and compare, for instance, Moses with David. What a difference of personality! Don't you think that David's personality comes out in his psalms? I do, but perhaps some will think it is wishful thinking on my part. However, I think David's personality is stamped on his own psalms. It is there. Moses had a personality and it comes out in the way he records things and in the way he sets things down. Jacob is an entirely different man from the other two with a difference of personality. Here you have three men who are entirely different.

If we compare Jeremiah and Daniel, what a difference in personality! They were great personalities. Jeremiah was a much more sensitive and artistic personality. He was either up in the heavens or down in the depths, and you knew it. When he was up in the heavens, you knew it, and when he was down in the depths, you knew it. Jeremiah is one of the people who has written some things that no one else in the Scriptures ever dared to say about the Lord, when he was down in the depths, some of the things he felt about the Lord, the way of the Lord and dealings with the Lord. He is up and he is down.

However, when you come to Isaiah, you sometimes wonder if Isaiah ever had a bad time. When you read through Isaiah and Jeremiah you find the difference. Jeremiah says, "I do not know why I have been called. The Lord has done this to me and done that to me." But when Isaiah speaks, you would hardly know Isaiah was there. It is the difference of personality. I am afraid Jeremiah is a bit more of an exhibitionist in one way, naturally and rightly. Isaiah is not an exhibitionist; he keeps himself out of the picture.

Daniel brings himself into the picture in quite a different way to Jeremiah. He speaks of himself being sick for a long time over a certain vision he had. He says it made his head sick, and he was very bad about it for quite a while. Daniel speaks about himself and records how he was brought in, how he was the key man in the end and how he rose to a great position. Yet it is quite different from Jeremiah. These are three personalities, absolutely different, but all of whom have left their stamp upon what they have given us. So there is God-breathed-out Scripture, and yet you have human personality.

Take Luke and John, two personalities that come out clearly in the writing of their Gospels. You cannot mix up Luke and John. Luke has got just the personality that is his and you find it both in Luke and the Acts. John had a personality, which is entirely different, and you find it in his writings.

We have already mentioned Paul, James and Peter, three distinct personalities. They all have left an indelible stamp upon what is called God-breathed-out Scripture. Once again we are in the presence of mystery. Somehow or other the personality of these writers is not obliterated by divine inspiration at all. If anything it is enhanced.

I do not know if you have ever noticed Revelation 1:9, summed up in the little word that John says, "I John," a thing many of us would be afraid to do because of being unspiritual. Paul, not once but quite a number of times said, "I Paul," quite unashamedly. Here is human personality indwelt by the Holy Spirit and rightly, and somehow the divine and the human aspect blend and the result is Scripture.

At times it would almost seem that the very failings of the individual, or perhaps we should more rightly say, their temperamental lack, is used by God. I have said that Paul has a propensity for abundance of language. I think if anything we would say that Paul, if we knew him in some way, was a little verbose in his writing. He stuttered evidently or had some speech trouble when he spoke, but in his writing he was really tremendous. He was very free. Paul was the kind of man who evidently was not afraid of just speaking out of his heart. And I am quite sure that if Paul were here, many a person here and in many other companies would have been most worried about him. Some would have said he should not open his heart like that and say that kind of thing; he really shouldn't. But read his letters, especially the second letter to the church at Corinth, some of the personal things he says. Do you see what I am getting at? It is very interesting because it says the Lord uses perhaps a point where there could be a little bit of trouble. It was a temperamental lack. It was the weakness of his constitution. Generally the good point of our temperament gives rise to its worst point.

Again with James, I expect he tended to legalism, and yet the Lord uses him. It seems that the Lord uses a bad thing about him. In the same way Jeremiah, who sometimes would sink into the depths, the Lord used it. All these men had one thing in common: they were chosen, apprehended, prepared, and anointed by the same Lord as vessels through which He would produce the Scriptures.

Conscious of Inspiration?

Were they always conscious and aware of being inspired? I wonder. It would seem from 1 Peter 1:10–11, that they were aware of it. It says, "The prophets sought and searched diligently, who prophesied of the grace that should come unto you: searching what time or what manner of time the Spirit of Christ which was in them did point unto, when it testified beforehand the sufferings of Christ and the glories that should follow them."

It was revealed to them that they were serving not themselves, but you. Now it would seem from that they were conscious of this inspiration. But just wait, were they? If you look at John 8:56, Jesus said about Abraham: "Your father Abraham rejoiced to see my day;

and he saw it, and was glad." That suggests that Abraham knew a good deal more about this dispensation than some of us would credit him with.

Then again in Galatians 3:8, you get another little side light on the Old Testament saints. "And the scripture, foreseeing that God would justify the Gentiles by faith, preached the gospel beforehand unto Abraham, saying, In thee shall all the nations be blessed." It suggests that he actually understood what the Lord meant when He said, "In thee shall all the nations be blessed." The Holy Spirit revealed to him what its meaning was. Is that so? It would seem so from this.

When you read through Hebrews 11, especially verses 13–16, you would feel that these men saw a good deal more than we think they did. They understood a good deal more. It says they inquired, they explored and they asked the Spirit within them what He meant by this prophecy.

There are other things which we question as in Acts 2. It says, speaking of David, it is clear that he spoke as the prophet who knew that God had sworn to him that one of his own direct descendants would sit on His throne. When he said, "He was not abandoned to Hades and his flesh never suffered corruption," he spoke with foreknowledge of the resurrection of the Messiah. It seems quite clear that David understood what he was talking about.

On the other side, what about Job? Was Job conscious in his experience that Scripture was in the making and something was happening? I do not know. What about Jonah? I do not believe for a moment that at the time Jonah knew that something was being worked out in his life that was going to be recorded and put into God's Word. These men didn't realise that. It was probably after they were gone that much of it actually began to take shape in its literary form.

Did David really understand when he first had that experience recorded in Psalm 22: "My God, my God, why hast Thou forsaken me?" Did he really understand it was the Messiah that it was talking of? These are questions.

Psalm 51 is David's confession of his fall with Bathsheba. A year passed away during which he would not confess his sin. Finally, he was convicted of it and put it right, and Psalm 51 was written. Do you think that David ever realised that psalm would become one of the greatest helps to Christians of all the psalms in the Psalter? Do you think he knew?

Then take dear Paul. Do you think Paul knew when he was writing some of these letters that in fact they were going to become part of what we call the New Testament? One of the most amusing parts I find in the whole New Testament is II Corinthians 7:8: "For though I made you sorry with my epistle, I do not regret it: though I did regret it." It is very interesting that here you have a man who regretted writing divinely inspired Scripture. He had a very bad time about his first letter, when in fact it was the Word of God. Isn't that interesting? Was he aware at the time that the Holy Spirit in him was breathing out something? Think of the first letter to Corinth. Forget the murky part of it in the earlier chapters, although they are wonderful, the first chapter of the first letter is wonderful. But think of the 12th chapter, the 13th chapter, and the 15th chapter. Nevertheless, Paul had such a bad time after he had sent that letter off and wished he had never written it. I have no doubt he thought: "That is just me again and my words have run away with me. I have gone too far, and now what is going to happen?

It will probably be the end of everything; it will just break their back. It is too much; I have been too severe with them." Yet, when the news finally got to him, he realised—and all was well.

I have just put this to you as a question. Were they always aware that they were divinely inspired? Do you think when Paul wrote the letter to Philemon he really knew that it was going to find its way into God's Word? Or when he wrote the first letter to the church at Thessalonica, and unfortunately they all took it very much to heart, which was a good thing normally, but in this case they took it far too much to heart. A lot of them gave up their jobs, sold their homes and everything and waited for the Lord to appear. When Paul heard about it, he was absolutely horrified and he dashed off a letter to tell them: Whatever you do you are going too far. Of course, you must not understand from my letter that the Lord is coming back right now; it is quite a time off. Do you think at that time he realised that those two letters were going to find their way into what we call the Bible? I think he would have thought perhaps of the Roman letter, but for others I think some of the spontaneity would have been restricted. Some of the humanity of God's Word would have been drawn back and we would have a kind of false and artificial spiritual overlay, which would not have been God. The amazing thing is this: until you and I are ourselves, God cannot be Himself. There is no place in which this is more true than in the Bible. These men were supremely what they were in God, and so they were not afraid. We have their weaknesses, their foibles, their failings, and their strong qualities; it is all there.

Divine Authorship

How can we summarise this matter? In all that we have said, the supreme thing about the Bible is its divine authorship. We are not handling something which merely contains God's Word nor something which merely breathes God. We are handling the Word of the Lord given us by divine inspiration. We may not fully understand the connection of divine inspiration with the human vessel, but it is true that if once you start to investigate Scripture you either have to throw it all overboard or you have got to come to this unqualified position that God is the Author of Scripture. An argument with Scripture invariably ends involving us with an argument with God. The Bible is the result of God breathing out His heart and mind by the Holy Spirit in certain men at different times. It is a God-given revelation of Himself, of His purpose, and of His salvation. It is just in that, that its unique and living authority and power lies. You cannot just admire God's Word, you cannot just play with God's Word, and you cannot just simply discuss God's Word. You have got to receive it through faith in obedience, humility, and reverence. Otherwise, it is a closed Book. In fact, it is more than a closed Book; it becomes confusing.

The Bible is a strange Book because either it opens its treasures by the Holy Spirit to you more and more or you become more and more confused and baffled. It either creates faith or it destroys faith, but there is no in between, and everything is dependent upon the attitude and mentality of our approach. So it is important for us to understand that we are handling the Word of the Lord. Human systems will rise and fall; great men will come and go. All flesh and all its glory is like the flowers of the field; they wither and fall, but the Word of the Lord endures forever. It is unchangeable. It is unshakeable. It is a sure and certain foundation upon which we can put our feet in Christ and know that we are safe.

May the Lord help every one of us to understand, from what we have said, a little more of the nature of this Book.

4.
The Theme of the Bible

The first thing I would like to say about the aim and scope of the Bible is that the Bible was never designed to cover the whole range of human knowledge in detail. Nor was it designed to be a revelation of all that could be revealed. There are some people who have an idea of the Bible, which while it exalts it and in some ways gives it its proper authority and place, yet it is false and leads more thinking people into many snares and disappointments. The Bible was never ever intended to cover the whole range of human knowledge. There is a sense in which the Bible of course does cover the whole range of human experience and knowledge, but it does not cover it in detail. It was never intended to do so, and certainly the Bible does not contain all that could be revealed by God. There is a vast and endless universe that could be revealed, but which God, in His wisdom and in His grace, has chosen not to reveal. The Bible is a God-given revelation and it has an aim and a scope, but it was never meant to cover the whole range of human wisdom.

Let's put it another way. The Bible is not an encyclopedia, not a divine encyclopedia, where you can turn the pages and find out everything about everything. It was never meant to be that. Nor is it a detailed history of the races and the nations. Nor is it, in fact, a history book of a particular nation or particular nations. It is not a book on astronomy or geology or botany or biology or zoology or any other "*ology.*" Again, that is not the scope of the Bible. It is not a handbook on science. Some people are disappointed with the Bible because they feel that it should be much more scientific than it is. Its aim rules that out, and we must understand that clearly. Nor is the Bible a philosophical treatise or a textbook on theology. I fear that some theologians have almost made the Bible into a kind of textbook for theology, but it was never intended to be a theological textbook. Philosophy or divine philosophy, of course, is in the Bible, but it is not a philosophical treatise. We must understand all of this.

If, in fact, the Bible had been any of these, its whole aim would have been seriously obscured if not wholly frustrated. Furthermore, the vast majority of mankind would have found the Bible wholly unintelligible. For instance, those who would like the Bible to be couched in much more scientific language would have discovered that the vast majority of mankind all down through the ages would have found the Bible a closed book to them. They would not have been able to understand it. Even today when you take the whole population of the world, there is only a tiny portion that would be able to understand the Bible whereas, in fact, the Bible can speak to every man and woman of every generation that has ever lived. That again is something we have to understand.

The Bible's Accuracy

Where the Bible touches upon anything in any field, it does so with absolute accuracy, and in the end it has always been vindicated. The Bible has been held up to ridicule, not just in the last century or two, but down through the centuries of time. Again and again, in different statements, different things that have been categorically stated in the Word of God have been held up to human ridicule. However, in the end the Bible has outlived the ridicule. Indeed, it has turned the tables upon those who have ridiculed it and made them appear ridiculous. There have been some very foolish things said, sometimes by learned men, which in the end have proved to be absolutely unfounded.

I think we ought to give one word of warning here. One has got to distinguish between clear and dogmatic statement of fact and poetry. For instance, what if I were to write a poem, (you won't find this in Scripture) and say, "This evening the stars hung like dew from threads of silver in the sky." No one would think that I actually believe that the stars were drops of dew hanging on silver threads in space. You would understand straightaway that I was being poetic and that when you look at the stars on a somewhat cold and frosty night they do look rather like drops of dew on threads of silver. Or if I spoke of the stars being like hoarfrost scattered through the heavens, again it may be a description, but I am not actually suggesting that the stars are all hoarfrost scattered through the heavens, a kind of heavenly hoarfrost. It is obvious that it is poetry. There are parts of God's Word in which there is true poetry and we have to understand it in its right setting and its right context. But wherever the Bible makes a clear and definite statement, it is unfailingly, unerringly accurate. Even when at the time men do not understand it and it seems to run contrary to the opinions then prevalent amongst men.

The Timelessness of the Bible's Language

Because the Bible has a definite aim, it uses popular language and modes of thought. Yet, it is a remarkable fact that such usage has proved timeless in its value. The Bible has always used popular language and the modes of thought common to the common man, and because of that it has a timelessness in its language. For instance, a child of God in David's day could read a verse from the book of Deuteronomy, and a child of God in Paul's day could read the same verse, and a child of God in Luther's day could read the same verse, and a child of God in our day could read the same verse and all four receive a blessing out of the same verse because of the timelessness of the language used. That is a point to bear in mind.

Let's look at it another way. Think of a primitive savage just recently saved, taught his language just recently reduced to script, reading a verse in a psalm for the first time in a faltering, stumbling way. He can have the same overwhelming sense of meeting with God in that psalm as a highly educated westerner reading a psalm. Somehow God's Word has been couched in such simplicity of popular language that God can speak to a savage who has come to Christ and a very highly educated and sophisticated man and reach both at the same moment. There is no other book that can do that. And if in fact this Bible had been written in any other kind of language or if other modes of thought had been used, it would never have reached the wide range of people, not only today, but all through time. I think we ought to take note of that.

Then, we ought to also add that the Bible is not a book of sermon outlines. I fear sometimes some ministers look upon the Bible as a divine book of ideas for sermons or illustrations for sermons, a book you sort of thumb through to find a really good illustration to prop up some thought you may have. Nor is it a mere divine promise box, as some Christians, especially Christian ladies, tend to use the Bible. Of course, it is absolutely true that all the promises in Christ are "yea and Amen," but the Bible is not *merely* a divinely inspired promise box for the use of Christians. Nor is it a kind of daily homily, daily thoughts, a book that you dig into every morning before you go to work to get a little treasure. Of course, mind you, it is vital and necessary to get something out of God's Word every day, but that is not the whole aim of the Bible, just to provide you with something each day. I am quite sure that is part of God's intention because it is necessary for you and I to be fed on the Word of God, but that is not the aim of the Bible. Nor is the Bible a collection of comforting scriptures, a whole lot of passages brought together which we just find helpful in times of trouble. Now, it may contain all of these various things we have mentioned, but they do not constitute the aim of the Bible.

The Bible's Aim and Scope

The Bible has a very clear and definite aim and everything revealed in it is related to that end. Its aim governs its scope. In Deuteronomy 29:29 it says, "The secret things belong unto the Lord our God; but the things that are revealed belong unto us and to our children for ever, that we may do all the words of this law." We must not expect to find in the Bible what is not important for us to know. On the other hand, everything which is vitally important for us is revealed within its pages. Its aim governs its scope. The Bible has a definite aim, therefore it does not become a treatise on geology or botany or biology or zoology or any of the other *ologies*. It touches science, of course, because science is part of life itself, but it is not a handbook on it. Its aim governs its scope. As mentioned before the Bible has a very definite aim; therefore everything which does not come into a vital relationship to that aim, or is not somehow or other furthering that aim, or helping us to understand that aim to be achieved in our lives or in our life together, is ruled out.

I am sure you can see quite obviously that if God had wanted to do so, He could have not merely given us sixty-six books but three hundred and sixty-six books. He could have gone on and on and on. The wealth of material we would have received would have completely overwhelmed us to such a degree that I think the real theme of the Bible would have been lost. We have had enough trouble, if I may say it reverently, with the sixty-six books that constitute this library. Volumes have been written, controversy has raged, conflicting ideas have stemmed from different interpretations of parts of this Book. Yet we believe that within these covers is the minimum that is absolutely necessary for us to understand. Everything here within these covers is vital to us if the aim of this Book is to be achieved in our individual lives and in our life together. This Book has had a job to do, not only in your life personally, but in all the lives of God's children from the beginning until now. Both while in the making, since it has been completed, and on until the last day dawns, this Book has a job to do and in

God's wisdom He has revealed certain things. Those things belong to us, but the rest He has drawn a veil over, and some of them are fascinating and entrancing. We would love to know some of the things which God has decided to keep secret. However, here in His Word He has revealed to us enough for us to understand what His purpose is, what He wants, how He is going to achieve it, and how you and I may be brought into it. So I want to repeat again and again that the aim governs the scope.

The Unity of the Bible's Theme

The aim of the Bible is remarkably evidenced in its unity of theme, which once seen is apparent everywhere in the books of the Bible. The Bible is like an immense tree. Its one life is variously manifested in roots here, and trunk there, the branches there with leaves and blossoms and fruit. The Bible has only one life, yet this immense tree, which is the Bible, somehow or other contains all kinds of manifestations of that one life. I look upon the life in the tree as the theme, and you see it everywhere under different guises. All of it is livingly connected, and every part of it is essential to the whole. The blossoms are essential to the whole tree. The leaves, the branches, and the roots are essential to the whole tree, and all have a part to play. They are manifestations of the life of the tree, different manifestations of the one life.

The Bible is just like that. It is like an immense tree in which there is one theme from beginning to end, and it is variously manifested in different parts of God's Word. So often when we are babes in Christ, we see the blossom, or we may see the leaves, or we may see the branches, but we fail to see the common source, the common life, and the common power of the whole. When we are young in the Lord and begin to read the Bible, we are perhaps taken up with things such as the second coming of the Lord; it thrills us. Matthew 24 is wonderful, and then, of course, there are chapters in Thessalonians about the coming of the Lord, and they fascinate us. How do they tie up?

Then, perhaps a little later we are absorbed with something else. Perhaps we are going through a troubled time in our lives, and somehow one of the psalms becomes alive to us and means so much to us at that time. Or perhaps we have started to read the life of Abraham, and that is something that means everything to us. Or maybe we have some Bible studies on the tabernacle. We marvel at how God designed the tabernacle and what each part symbolises, but we fail to see the theme that runs throughout the whole Book. We see the various parts and we are thrilled and helped by the various parts, but we do not come to see the essential theme that runs throughout.

Comparing Genesis and Revelation

Now, in understanding the aim of the Bible we have got to realise that it is contained throughout and it is variously manifested. There is a relationship between the first three chapters of Genesis[1] and the last three chapters of the book of Revelation. It is remarkable that this Book we call the Bible has an introduction and a conclusion, and that introduction and conclusion completely concur; they correspond. It is the beginning of something and its conclusion, its finalisation, its realisation. It is an even more remarkable fact

1 See chart on following pages

that if you were to take the first two chapters of Genesis and the last two chapters of Revelation, it is without sin. The only reference to it would be no more pain, crying or death, and the fact that nothing that defiles or makes an abomination can enter into the city. That would be the only inference that there had been something unclean or sinful. In fact, you would have the beginning of something and the end of something.

In other words, you will have, as it were, what God originally intended and the way God has got it. In the first three chapters— heaven and earth, and the last three chapters—a new heaven and a new earth. In the first three chapters—paradise lost, and in the last three chapters—paradise regained. In the first three chapters Satan enters; in the last three chapters Satan is cast out forever and ever. In the first three chapters earth is cursed; in the last three chapters there is no more curse. In the first three chapters there are two human beings—Adam and Eve, and note the progression here. In the last three chapters they have become a redeemed people that no man can number. In the first three chapters there is a garden, and again, note a progression. In the last three chapters the garden has become a city, a garden city, but it is a city. In the first three chapters there is the tree of life in the midst of the garden; in the last three chapters there is the tree of life in the midst of the city. In the first three chapters there is the river whose source is in the garden, and which becomes four great rivers that water the earth; and in the last three chapters we have the river of life which proceeds out of the throne of God, out of the midst of the city. In the first three chapters God is walking in the midst of the garden at a certain time each day; He came into the garden to commune with man and woman. In the last three chapters God is "at home."

First Three Chapters of the Bible

Heaven and Earth	Genesis 2:4
Time Ushered in	Genesis 1
Satan Enters	Genesis 3:1
Paradise Lost	Genesis 3:24
Earth Cursed	Genesis 3:17
Adam and Eve	Genesis 3:23
A Garden	Genesis 2:8
The Tree of Life	Genesis 2:9
The River of Life	Genesis 2:10
God walking in the midst (once per day)	Genesis 3:8
Earthly Marriage (man and woman)	Genesis 2:21-25
Pain, Sorrow, Death	Genesis 3:16-19
Gold, Precious Stone, Pearl	Genesis 2:11-12
The Spirit of God "Brooding"	Genesis 1:2

Notes:

Onyx stone is used in the Bible to represent precious stone. Exodus 28:9-12 cf 28:18-20, 29

Bdellium – A plant which when broken exudes a substance that dries into the colour and shape of a pearl.

In Gen 1:2 "moved upon," literally "hovering" (as an eagle) or "brooding".

Last Three Chapters of the Bible	
New Heaven and New Earth	Revelation 21:1
Eternity Ushered in	Revelation 21
Satan Cast Out Forever	Revelation 20:10
Paradise Regained	Revelation 21:3
No More Curse	Revelation 22:3
A Redeemed People	Revelation 21:3; 22:14
A City	Revelation 21:2
The Tree of Life	Revelation 22:2
The River of Life	Revelation 22:1
God walking in the midst (forever)	Revelation 21:3
Heavenly Marriage (the Lamb & the Wife)	Revelation 21:2
No More Pain, Crying, Mourning or Death	Revelation 21:4
Gold, Precious Stone, Pearl	Revelation 21:18-21
The Spirit & the Bride saying "Come"	Revelation 22:17

He dwells forever in the midst of the city. He is not visiting at a certain time; He is there forever. He will make His tabernacle a home with men as it says in Revelation 21:3.

In the first three chapters of Genesis there is an earthly marriage—Adam and Eve are wed. In the last three chapters there is a heavenly marriage—the Lamb and the wife of the Lamb are wed together. In the first three chapters there are pain, sorrow and death. In the last three chapters there is no more pain, crying, mourning, or death. In the first three chapters time is ushered in, and in the last three chapters eternity is ushered in. In the first three chapters we have the mysterious but significant mention of three materials—gold, bdellium, and onyx stone (see Genesis 2:11-12). If you follow the course of the river you will find gold, bdellium [precious] stone, and the onyx stone. In Exodus we find that the high priest had twelve precious stones on his breastplate, and on each stone was engraved one of the tribes of the children of Israel. On his shoulders he had two blocks of precious stone, which were onyx stones, and on each shoulder he had six names. In other words, the onyx stones symbolized all the precious stones on the breastplate of the high priest.

Then there was the bdellium which was an aromatic plant, and when the branch was broken, a white substance oozed out which quickly hardened. The rabbis in Christ's day had always discussed what this meant. Many of them were of the conviction that it was a pearl because it was found in the river as you followed its course. We do not know whether it was an actual pearl or whether it was just something that when it was broken and became hard looked like a pearl. In Hebrew, the tree being almost the same as the plant is called the pearl plant. When you get to the last three chapters of the book of Revelation, you discover that the city has been produced out of only three materials, gold, precious stone, and pearl. The interesting thing is that in the first three chapters the gold, precious stone, and the pearl are all hidden. You have to follow the course of the river to find the precious materials. However, when you come to the last three chapters, these materials have not only been discovered but they have been worked upon, refined, and polished and they have become a city. There are only three materials out of which the city is produced. Of course, we know it is only symbolic, but the city is produced out of only three materials: gold, precious stone, and pearl.

In the first three chapters we have the Spirit of God brooding. In Genesis 1:2 it says, "And the Spirit of God moved upon the face of the waters," or in the margin of the Revised Version it says, "The Spirit was brooding upon the face of the waters." The Hebrew word used is the word that came from an eagle or vulture when it was hovering, waiting. The Holy Spirit was, as it were, hovering, looking around, taking in everything or seeking to find either a place to land or what it was going to do next. This is the picture we have of the Spirit of God in the first verses of the Bible. He is brooding upon the face of the waters. Later on, of course, we discover that out of all the chaos and the void He produces something. But the first picture we ever get, if I may use it almost irreverently, is of the anxiety and agitation of the Holy Spirit of God. In the last three chapters of the Bible, almost the last verses, there is a different picture altogether. It is a most remarkable phrase when you think about it. You would have thought it would have said, "The Lord Jesus and the bride say, Come." Instead, we have "The Spirit and the bride say, Come." It is as if the Holy Spirit was brooding over the whole of world history from eternity to eternity, and what He was moving upon has finally been produced out of much conflict and battle. Now the Holy Spirit has the bride at His side, and so it is He is saying to the whole of mankind, "Now the objective of God is realized: Come, the door is now open to a new era. All that God originally intended has been achieved."

Of course, we do not know what eternity to come holds. All we know is that the Spirit and the bride say, "Come." It is a very wonderful picture that in the first three chapters of the Bible you have the Spirit of God brooding, hovering upon the face of the waters. But in the last three chapters you have the Spirit taking John, not an angel, but the Spirit taking John into a high place and showing him the holy city, the wife of the Lamb coming down out of heaven. In the last recorded utterance, the Spirit and the bride say, "Come."

I am quite sure that it is in an understanding of the relationship between the first three chapters of the Bible and the last three chapters of the Bible that we come to an understanding of the aim of the Bible. I do not know whether you do as some of us do to discover what a book is about. We read the first few pages and the last few pages just to get an idea of what exactly the character and purpose of the book is. I am quite sure that as we reflect upon and study the first three chapters and the last three chapters of the Bible, you and I will come to an understanding of what is the aim of the Bible.

The Origin and Conclusion of the Bible

Here is a little design that puts the whole Bible in a nutshell: origins—Genesis; issues—Revelation; processes—Exodus to Jude.

Origins	Processes	Issues
Genesis	Exodus-Jude	Revelation

It is so simple. Of course, when you really look into it, it is not quite as simple as that. Nevertheless, just as a sort of bird's eye view of the whole Bible, Genesis is a book of origins. There is nothing in the whole Bible that does not find its origin in the book of Genesis. The book of Revelation is a book of issues; it is not just like the other books. It is a book of the conclusions of things. Everything has come to its final consummation. For instance, you have fallen man at the very zenith of his power. You have Babylon, that great city which is the symbol of man in all his creative genius and all his fallen energy and power. On the other side you have the city of God coming to its fulfillment. You have the harlot on one side and the bride on the other side. You have got this amazing picture of the issues of everything. You have God working out His purpose and coming to the climax of it, and you have Satan working out his design and purpose and coming to the climax of it. There are two sides—God, as it were, bringing everything to its climax in the appearing of Jesus Christ for the second time, and the devil bringing everything to its climax in the appearance of the antichrist, the man of sin, the beast, and the false beast. The kingdom of God is ripening for its appearance upon the stage of time and eternity. On the other side you have the ripening of a world system, which goes right back into the mists of antiquity, also coming to its fulfillment.

I would like you to mark some other things about the Bible. I have said that the aim of the Bible is evidenced in its unity. This unity is seen in many, many ways. It is rather interesting that the Bible begins with God in Genesis 1:1: "In the beginning God ..."

And it is rather beautiful that the Bible ends with the saints. The very last word in the whole Bible, except for Amen, is: "The grace of the Lord Jesus be with the saints." It is also interesting that in the very central verses of the Bible, Psalm 118:7–9, we find God and man reconciled. "The Lord is on my side among them that help me: Therefore, shall I see my desire upon them that hate me. It is better to take refuge in the Lord than to put confidence in man. It is better to take refuge in the Lord than to put confidence in princes."

It is rather remarkable that the Bible begins with God, ends with man, and its central verses are God and man reconciled into one.

It is also rather interesting that the first question ever asked in the Old Testament is the question that God asked of man: "Where art thou?" (Genesis 3:9), and the first question in the New Testament is asked by men of God: "Where is he?" (Matthew 2:2).

The Bible's Basic Themes

Then again, I think we should be greatly helped if we understand the basic themes in Scripture, for there are many which all flow into the one great theme. We will look at each one and then sum it up and see if we can come to the major theme of the Bible. They are like many tributaries running into a great river.

Atonement Through Blood

The first theme is this matter of atonement through blood and we can see it from Genesis to Revelation. It is one of the most remarkable strands running right through the Bible. It begins in Genesis 3:21, right in the watershed of the Bible: "The Lord God made for Adam and his wife coats of skins, and clothed them." That was the first time that blood was ever shed in human history. Man and woman had fallen, and they tried to cover their nakedness with leaves which they themselves stitched. But God showed them that the only way their sin could be atoned for was by the terrible way of death, the shedding of blood. In other words, there had to be a death for sin in order that there might be an atonement made for sin.

Immediately, in chapter 4 as if to enforce the lesson, we find the story of Abel and Cain. Cain tried to bring again the fruits of the ground, which in the Bible are always a symbol of man's natural works. He tried to bring this to God as an offering to God, something, as it were, to cover himself before God. Abel brought a lamb and Abel's offering was accepted, but Cain's was rejected. Then follows the story that because of Cain's hatred of Abel because he was accepted by God, he slew him. Here you have again this whole matter of the atonement through blood. God rejected Cain because he did not bring a lamb; instead he brought the works of his hands.

When we come to the book of Exodus, chapters 12, 13, and 14, we have the Exodus, the Passover, one of the great themes of Scripture. It began as a little trickle in Genesis 3, it began to broaden out in Genesis 4, and as you trace it all the way through Genesis it becomes a real rivulet. By the time it comes to Exodus 12, 13, and 14, it has become a river. Now, for the first time it is becoming clear. There can be no passing over of sin unless there is the shedding of the blood of a lamb. That lamb's blood has got to be put on the lintels of the door. The mark has got to be on the outside, and the lamb itself has got to be consumed, has got to be eaten by those who are within the house.

As we go on from there, we come to all the sacrifices of the book of Leviticus—trespass offerings, sin offerings, whole burnt offerings, peace offerings, and meal offerings. All of these offerings speak again of atonement through blood. The only way to come into the presence of God is by the shedding of blood for the atonement of our sin.

Then there is the question of prophecy, and of course we have Isaiah 53. What might seem to be crude and almost repulsive to our natural mind, suddenly takes on a new light. In Isaiah 53:5–6 we are told: "But he was wounded for our transgressions, he was bruised for our iniquities; the chastisement of our peace was upon him; and with his stripes we are healed. All we like sheep have gone astray; we have turned everyone to his own way; and the Lord has laid on Him the iniquity of us all ... (v7) He was led as a sheep to the shearers." It goes on and on until for the first time, hundreds and hundreds of years before Christ's coming and work, we have a full-orbed view that all the shedding of blood was only a foreshadowing of Him who was to be the Lamb of God, who by the shedding of His own blood was to bear away the sin of the whole world.

In Psalm 22 we have come to the heart of the matter. Here is another passage that speaks of the shedding of blood, but it is the shedding of Christ's blood: (v1) "My God, my God, why hast Thou forsaken me?" When you read through this psalm, you understand that the purpose of God is centered in the work of Christ on the cross.

In Zechariah 13:6 we read these mysterious words about "the wounds in the midst of thy hands." What do you think? Again, it is speaking of the sacrifice of Christ for our sins. This atonement theme in the Bible was hundreds of years before Christ came, but we have this amazing picture. We are told in Zechariah 13:7 about "the sword awaking against the man who is my fellow, says the Lord." This quotation cannot refer to anyone else but Christ, for none of us are the "fellow," the equal of God.

When we come to the New Testament, immediately we are at the heart of the matter. "Christ Jesus came into the world to save sinners," says Paul (1 Timothy 1:15). The Father sent the Son to be the Savior of the world. "For God so loved the world that He gave His only begotten Son" (John 3:16). You have the heart of the matter in the teaching of Christ and the teaching of the apostles. Calvary is a theme from beginning to end of the Bible.

Everywhere you turn in the Epistles, whether it is in the letters of Paul, or Peter, or James, or the writer of the Hebrews, you are up against the cross. Everywhere it is the cross. Then you come to the book of Revelation, and you think perhaps you are finished with Calvary, but there at the heart of eternity to come, you see a Lamb as it had been slain. This atonement theme of the slain Lamb begins in Genesis and runs right the way through to the book of Revelation.

God's Dwelling Place

Let's consider another theme in God's Word: God's dwelling place, for want of a better word, or God's home. Here is another theme in Scripture—the home of God. It begins in Genesis and ends in the book of Revelation. Of course, it does not really end in the book of Revelation, but that is where we lose sight of it. As far as we are concerned, it concludes there.

Right back to Genesis 2, we see Adam being put to sleep. Out of his side some flesh and bone were taken, and we see woman being formed out of Adam, then brought to him. Adam said, "This is now flesh of my flesh and bone of my bone. She shall be called woman because she was taken out of man" (Genesis 2:23). Then he goes on to say, "These two shall become one flesh" (v24). Now this is the beginning of what we call marriage. But marriage in itself, as the marriage service so beautifully states it, is "until death do us part." It is a temporary thing. It ends with death when we pass into another life, another way altogether. It is something temporary and for this life because marriage was instituted—as the old state church service puts it—to signify the mystery of the union betwixt Christ and His church. There you find the norm of this whole matter of the home of God—a man and a woman becoming one, a man and a woman finding their home, one in the other, a man and a woman becoming two parts of one whole. Now God says, "This is what I want."

Here begins a story which you can trace right through until you come to the book of Exodus, to a nation. Adam and Eve had become a people which became a huge multitude, and God made a covenant with them and sealed it with blood. We are told that this covenant relationship is marriage. God says to the children of Israel, "This day I have married you." From that point on in the Bible God's children are looked upon as the wife of the Lord, as the bride of God. Right the way through this is the great cry of the prophets. When they find that God's people are sinning and compromising, they did not call it compromise; they called it adultery. That is the word they used because God's people had left their own husband

and were having love affairs with others. So the prophets call compromise, worldliness, and mixture adultery.

You find the summing up of this thing in the prophet Hosea. In the book of Hosea you have the most wonderful cry from the heart of God about this faithless bride of His. Hosea had this experience himself. He had a wife that he bought in the slave market, and he redeemed her. She proved to be faithless, and it broke his heart until he went and found her again.

The point that we are making is that here in God's Word is this theme running right the way through. In Ephesians, chapter 5, Paul has quite a lot to say to husbands and wives, but he does not just say it to them as husbands and wives. He says it to them because they are a picture of Christ and the church. His whole attitude is that there is an awful lot here to be said just because this matter has been lifted onto an altogether new level.

As we go on to Revelation, chapters 20–21, we have the last concluding words about this matter when you see the wife of the Lamb, the holy city, the New Jerusalem coming down out of heaven. There is a marriage feast. That is the end and she is entering now into her married life with the Lamb.

This question of a home for God is not only spoken under the symbol of a bride, or a wife. It is found in the tabernacle, which occupies such a large place in the early part of the Old Testament. Or again, it is found under the symbol of the temple which occupies such a large place in the latter part of the Old Testament. These two terms, tabernacle and temple, constitute a whole area of the Old Testament. So you see this theme—the bride, the tabernacle, the temple—is all the same thing running right through Scripture.

When we come to the New Testament, it is all transferred to what the Lord Jesus called, "My church; upon this rock I will build My church." So this whole theme runs throughout Scripture, whether it is used under the symbol of bride, tabernacle, temple, the body of Christ, or the city of God. Throughout Scripture it is the home of God, and it is another theme in God's Word.

The History of God's People

When you follow the history of God's children, there is another theme from beginning to end. There is a history in God's Word right the way through the Old Testament and the New Testament. It begins in Eden with the original intention of God in the creation of man and it goes on after His great offer of the probation that man was put under. He could either have the tree of life or he could have the tree of the knowledge of good and evil. Man chose the tree of the knowledge of good and evil, and what we call "the fall" took place. Something came into man's very being that was alien to God. Man became another creature to that which God intended. His very constitution was altered. The very image of God was defaced, and somehow or other a satanic element became wedded to man. Satan fathered the human race and from that point on there are two things. You have what the Quakers called "the good seed and the bad seed." Right the way through the Bible, we can begin to trace these two streams both beginning in the first chapters of Genesis. One is the course of evil, fallen man, and the other is the course of a new man, redeemed man.

All the way through Scripture we can follow the course. We are not going to follow the course of fallen man, but very swiftly we can follow the course of redeemed man. Out of the Garden of Eden we follow them through Enoch who was translated, through Noah and the building of the ark, and the flood which destroyed the whole world except eight being saved out of it. He is dealing with mankind just simply as races and nations.

Then we go on to Abraham, where we come to a new phase in God's purpose. He calls out one man, Abraham, and tells him that he going to become the father of all who believe. Out from Abraham come Isaac and Jacob, and Jacob has twelve sons who become the fathers of the children of God, the children of Israel. Then we see Joseph going down into Egypt and then being raised up in the most remarkable way to provide for all the others. They all go down to Egypt where they remained for many centuries until they become a strong nation.

Then comes the era of Moses, and we discover the man that God has equipped to lead out a nation and care for them. There is the birth of a nation in the Passover and the Exodus. The people of God and of the old covenant were born by blood and by water. They were born by the blood of the Passover lamb and by the water of the Red Sea. We trace their course right the way through the wilderness where the Law was given to them and God revealed Himself. The tabernacle was given to them, and they had a picture of the house of God. We go on right the way through until we come into the Promised Land and we watch Joshua lead the people over into the possession of the Promised Land where they settled.

When we come to the time of Samuel it is a new phase in the history of God's children. We begin to see the introduction of the throne. God's people choose a king, but a false king, and then they are led to the right king, David. Then we come to the temple and the zenith of the history of God's people in the Old Testament, the reign of Solomon. After that there is the exile, the restoration, and the time of the prophets. The whole is one unfolding history of God's dealings with a community of redeemed people, redeemed by blood.

As we come to the Lord Jesus Christ in the first chapters of Matthew, we discover that here is One who is Himself the fulfillment of the whole of the Old Testament. From then on we begin to follow another course. We watch Him in His great life and His ministry. We begin to see how all of the Scriptures in the Old Testament, both in word and in type, have been fulfilled in Him. Then we come to the cross where He offered Himself up, and on the third day the resurrection, and then the day of Pentecost, the birth of the church. We have had the shadow up until then. Now the substantial has come and the shadow has given way to the real thing. The book of Acts is not finished; it is an unfinished record. As Dr. Campbell Morgan has pointed out, the story is not finished yet. We are still in the story of the history of God's dealings with this community of redeemed people going right back to Abel and on to the last one who will ever be redeemed by the blood of the Lamb. We are all in this wonderful community of the redeemed.

This whole idea is obscured in the English translations because in the Old Testament the word congregation is used and in the New Testament the word church is used. However, to the New Testament saints reading the Septuagint Version of the Old Testament, they had the same word ecclesia in both and they could see straight away that there was an ecclesia in the Old Testament and there is an ecclesia in the New Testament. The two are one. Here was a theme running through Scripture and the wonder of it all is that it is not finished. You and I are part of it. Where do we trace our origins? It is not to the day of Pentecost. We go back before the day of Pentecost. We go back to Solomon, to David, to Samuel, to Moses, on through Joseph and Jacob, back to Abraham, beyond Abraham to Noah and Enoch, and back to Abel. We are in a community of redeemed ones.

The Battle of the Ages over the Purpose of God

I think we ought to recognise that there is yet another theme, another of these tributaries that flow into the one great river, and it leads us to the major theme of Scripture. It is the great battle over the purpose of God. Psalm 2 is the most eloquent interpretation of this battle that has raged from eternity on to eternity to come. It is this battle over the purpose of God. Is God going to have His way or is He not? In this Book it is revealed to us that there was one who said, "I will be like the Most High. I will exalt my throne above the throne of God." Here then is the key to the conflict. There is a great adversary of God who has lifted up his hand against the Lord. Through time there has been the manifestation of a heavenly battle. This battle is simply whether God is going to reign. To put it another way, this word kingdom of God is what we are talking about. We get a slightly false idea with the word kingdom because it is a rather comprehensive word. We could say, "the rule of God" or "the reign of God." It is a question of whether God's reign is going to be established or not.

Jeremiah 17:12 is a key to the whole Bible in many ways. It says, "A glorious throne, set on high from the beginning, is the place of our sanctuary." The whole theme is here is this verse: "A glorious throne, set on high is the place of our sanctuary." In other words, right from the beginning, on to the end, the throne of God's glory is the place on high, that is the sanctuary of the redeemed. It is this which the enemy, the evil one, is out to frustrate and counter.

And in Psalm 2 there is this tremendous atmosphere of conflict. The nations are raging. Kings are meditating futile things. It is all against the Lord and against His Anointed, and it is rebellion. "Let us cast His bands asunder," they said. But the Lord's word is this: "Yet I have set my king upon my holy hill of Zion." Now that is the key to the Bible. God is on the throne and the Bible is a record of great systems that have risen up which are only the earthly, physical manifestation of something essentially spiritual which is satanic, and which has as its objective the dethronement of God and the enthronement of man. So, there is this great battle between God and Satan which fills the Biblical stage. The point is this: God is set in the midst of the battle, while the kings meditate futile, vain things, and while the nations rage, and whilst the rebellion is at its height, "He that sitteth in the heavens shall laugh. Yet I have set my king upon my holy hill of Zion."

God uses every single device of the enemy to work out in the end His own purpose. When you read on it says, "Ask of me, and I will give thee the nations for thine inheritance, and the uttermost parts of the earth for thy possession." Here is the key to the battle. When Jesus met the devil in the wilderness, the devil said to Him: "Bow to me, worship me, and I will give thee the kingdoms of the world" (Matthew 4:8–9). Jesus never contradicted him. Satan is the prince of this world and the kingdoms of this world belong to him. Paul speaks of it like this: "The world rulers of darkness." Who are they? Physical beings? No, he speaks of this: "We wrestle not against flesh and blood but against principalities and powers, world rulers of darkness, against hosts of wicked spirits in the heavenlies" (see Ephesians 6:12). It is a strange array; an invisible array behind what is physical and earthly. This is the battle.

Everywhere we look in the Bible, whether I and II Chronicles, Ezra and Nehemiah, after having told us the whole story, having a history already from the beginning, we take it right back to Adam and right on to the end of the Old Testament. Why can't the two books of Samuel and the two books of Kings do it for us? God wants to emphasize what the heart of this battle is and we see in those books it is the temple. That is the thing the battle is raging over.

We come to the Song of Solomon, and here you have an allegory which is a picture of God and His church. Here we find another kind of battle. She keeps getting so self-satisfied that her love for her Lord just vanishes. This is a story of love, a love story, but it is a battle all the same to wean her away from all that makes her self-sufficient and independent. The last story in that Song of Solomon is when the cry goes up: "Who is this coming up out of the wilderness leaning on her beloved?" She has learned her lesson. In the last chapters of the Song of Songs what does she say? "My beloved is mine and I am His." A little later on it is, "I am my Beloved and He is mine." A little later on it is, "I am my Beloved's." The rest is gone, and something has happened. It is no longer his and hers, in the last chapter of Song of Solomon it is ours. Something has happened.

This is in all the different parts of the Bible which speak essentially of God's purpose. In Revelation there is this great battle that rages over the purpose of God, and it begins with the churches. We see all their difficulties and all the collapse amongst the churches. Later, when we have moved on from the churches, we see the great battle between these two—Babylon and Jerusalem. Finally, you hear the great cry that goes up: "The kingdoms of this world have become the kingdom of God and of His Christ." Then that other great cry: "The marriage supper of the Lamb has come, and the bride has made herself ready."

The Bible's Three-fold Theme

All of this comes together to what is the major theme of the Bible, and it is simply that we have a three-fold theme in the Scriptures. There is the Savior, there is the method or the salvation, and there are the saved ones. You can put it in different ways. You can put it like this: the Redeemer, the redemption, and the redeemed. Or you can put it like this: the Mediator of the covenant, the blood of His covenant, and the people of the covenant. But you have this three-fold theme all the way through, and this is the explanation of Scripture from beginning to end. It does not matter how we put it. This three-fold theme is everywhere in the Word—Christ, the cross, His people. Christ is the One who is the centre, the heart of it all. The cross is the means by which He does everything. We as His people are those who are saved by Him through His cross. It is as simple as that.

It is in an understanding of this— that Christ is the key to it all, the center and the heart and the fulfillment of it all—that we shall come to an understanding of the aim and the scope of the Bible. The Bible is a revelation of God's eternal purpose with the supreme aim that we might be saved into it—a three-fold theme—the Redeemer, the redemption, and the redeemed. May the Lord help us.

The Relationship of the Eternal Purpose of God to the Redeeming Purpose of God		
The original intention of God and the fall	The Redeemer The work of redemption The redeemed	The original intention realised and the glory which follows
Genesis 1–3	Genesis to Revelation	Revelation 20–22
Note how the three-fold theme of the Bible begins in Genesis 1–3 and ends in Revelation 20–22, and how we are given the essential information concerning God's eternal purpose and His redeeming work necessary to our understanding and experience of it in the whole Bible.		

The Scope of the Bible

Before times
eternal
(just a glimpse)

The week of time
(the main focus)

Age to come
"the ages of ages"
(just a glimpse)

The Week of Time

| Probation | Conscience | Races | Patriarchs | The Law | Grace | The Millennium |

Creation → the fall → the flood → Abraham → Moses → Christ

5.
The Aim and Scope of the Bible

I want you to just see very simply the whole scope of the Bible. The scope is from before times eternal until the ages to come or the ages of the ages. You see time beginning at creation and ending at the coming of the city, the end of the millennium. I have divided it up, although there is a little bit of controversy over this, into the major seven days, the week of time, which is generally understood. There are those who have other ideas but generally these seven periods or ages, as we call them in Scripture, are more or less clearly defined. Some have more ages, and there are a few who have less than the seven. They have six because they have cut out the millennium. Otherwise, the others are agreed on by all.

Beginning with the creation, the period or age of probation, which ends with the fall.

The period or age of conscience, which ended with the flood.

The beginning and end of the age of the races, which ends with Abraham.

The patriarchal age, from Abraham to Moses.

The age of Law, from Moses to Christ.

The age of grace, which we are now in together.

Lastly, this seventh, called the rest of God normally, the seventh day of time.

Whatever you may feel about the ages, you can see that the scope of the Bible, generally, is from the beginning of time to the end of time. It only gives us a glimpse of before times eternal, a real glimpse, but nevertheless only a glimpse, and it gives us only a glimpse of the ages to come, a real glimpse, but nevertheless only a glimpse. Will you keep that in mind? Keep in mind that the Bible is a revelation of God's eternal purpose with the supreme aim that we might be saved into it.

Before we can really see what the theme of the Bible is, we ought to note a number of threads which run right the way through the whole of Scripture. There are five threads that run from Genesis to Revelation. The first is Christ, the promised Messiah, the seed of the woman, and it is found from Genesis right through to the book of Revelation.

The second thread is atonement through blood, beginning in the third chapter of Genesis and going right the way through the whole Bible until we come to the book of Revelation.

The third point is God's dwelling place, and again we discover it throughout the whole of the Bible under various figures. We find it in the symbol of the bride, of the tabernacle, of the temple, of the body, of the city, and so on. From the beginning to the end of the Bible there is the thread of God's dwelling place running through it.

Five Threads Running Through Scripture

	before creation	in Genesis: the seed of the woman	in age of Grace: Redeemer	in Revelation: seated on the throne
Christ	the Lamb slain before creation of the world		in age of Grace: Redeemer	in Revelation: seated on the throne
Atonement	Genesis 3: the atonement of blood animals slain & skins used for covering		age of probation on to Millenium we have atonement by blood of the Lamb	Revelation 1:5-6 loosed from sins by blood of Christ and made a kingdom
God's Dwelling	Tabernacle & Temple		Body of Christ becoming the Bride of Christ	City of God
History of God's People	Creation, "the good seed", & the fall	the flood to Abraham to Moses to Christ		Book of Acts continues on to the 2nd coming
The Adversary, Battle, and Triumph	before times eternal (before ages)		battle of the ages	God's triumph "Day of the Lord"

The fourth thread is the history of God's people from the beginning. The Bible traces as one of its themes, what the Quakers used to call, "the good seed." It began with Abel and is taken right through the whole of history until the present day. In fact, the book of Daniel and the book of Revelation foresee the triumph of God's own people, and in a strange way foretell the history of God's people. That is why many believe that the book of Acts is an unfinished record because it linked up the church in the Old Testament with the church in the New Testament. The most marvellous thing of all is that it ends on an unfinished note. The point being that all of us are part of the story of the Acts of the Apostles. Daniel and some of the other prophets, principally Daniel, and John in the book of Revelation, take up this thread and it is found there.

The fifth thread is the adversary of God, the battle of the ages, and God's triumph. Those are five threads that are found woven together from the beginning to the end of the Bible. Out of those five threads there emerges a three-fold theme—one Saviour, one salvation, and one company of the saved. It takes all of these five to reveal this three-fold theme that sums up the whole Bible—one Saviour, one salvation, one company of the saved. You can put it in different ways: for instance, one Mediator of the covenant, the blood of His covenant, and the people of the covenant. Or you could put it this way: the Bringer of salvation—the Savior, the way of salvation—Calvary, and the company of the saved—the saved. Or put it in an even simpler way, which is the one easiest to remember: the Redeemer, the redemption, and the redeemed. However you like to entitle it, there is a three-fold theme that runs like a great Amazon-like river from beginning to end of the whole Bible and takes the whole of it within its grasp.

Five Threads from Genesis to Revelation

You will find all of these five threads right from the very beginning in the Garden. Before times eternal, spoken of in Scripture, is the Lamb as it was slain before the foundation of the world. You have Christ, before times eternal, destined to become the Saviour of the world. After the fall you have the atonement through blood, the slaying of animals and the clothing with skins instead of leaves. From then on right the way through these different ages—the Age of Probation, the Age of Conscience, the Age of the Races, the Age of the Patriarchs, the Age of Law, and the Age of Grace, on into the Age of the Millennium—it is atonement through blood. It is not the blood of bulls and goats, but the blood of Christ, as of a Lamb without spot or without blemish. The whole of the Bible is taken up with atonement through blood, not the blood of animals, but the blood of God's own Son. Again, it commences in the heart of God before times eternal—the Lamb as it had been slain from before the foundation of the world. At the very end of the Bible, in the book of Revelation, we hear a great song coming from a great innumerable multitude speaking of the blood of Christ by which they have been loosed from their sins and made a kingdom of priests unto their God.

Then, in each of these ages we find that there is an unfolding revelation of what God really wants, this spiritual home that God is looking for, not made of bricks and stones, not a great institution or organisation, but of living stones, made up of redeemed men and women. When you come to the end of the Book, we find that God has got what He wanted. Through the cross, He has purchased this dwelling place and at the end He has it.

So it is also with the history of God's people. Right the way through the creation, the fall, the flood, Abraham, Moses, Christ, and the second coming—it is the history of God's people. Some of the books of the Bible in certain portions go right the way back to the beginning and trace it all the way through, as if it is giving us a survey; for instance I and II Chronicles does that. It goes right the way back to Adam and traces the whole history again, although we already have history in other parts of God's Word. It does it again for us because the whole point is that it wants to show us what is really the deepest objective of God's heart. It was not just to have a nation called the Jews, but to have a dwelling place amongst men. In the New Testament, the letter to the Hebrews does the same. It tries to explain to us something of what God's real thought is, not just to be saved, but to go on into the inheritance that is ours.

This other thread, the adversary of God, goes right back before times eternal. Right the way through there is this terrific battle of the ages. When we speak of the battle of the ages, we mean these ages. According to Scripture these are ages of time and are before times eternal, which is before the ages. Afterwards there are the ages to come and the ages of the ages, but these are the ages of time. Of course, not everyone will agree to the division into seven, but most will agree. Some do not agree with the last division because they do not quite see the millennium. They believe that one goes right on forever, the Sabbath rest. But the week of time, as it is commonly called, is agreed by nearly all Roman Catholic and Protestant theologians—the great week of time. Whether the last day of the week goes on forever into the final Sabbath rest of God and of man, that is the question.

This battle of the ages is a tremendous battle in which God and His great adversary are locked in as to who is going to be King and who is going to have the throne of the universe. Of course, we are in that battle; it is quite contemporary. The international scene today is but the outward evidence of a terrible battle which has been raging for generations and generations right through these ages and reaches a climax at the end of human history. We have not seen the worst yet; it is still to come.

Of course I am glad to say we have the end, which is God's triumph. This chart is the story not only of the adversary of God, Satan, and his host, and not only the battle of the ages, but it is the story of God's continual triumph. When everything seems at its darkest and blackest, God triumphs again and again. The Scriptures call it "the day of the Lord." There have been many days of the Lord when the Lord has come out on top and the enemy has gone down under. Of course it will all be summed up in the day of the Lord, that great day, as Scripture entitles it, which will be at the end, when God will finally and completely triumph. It will be the end of all this trouble that we are so used to.

The Three-fold Theme of the Bible

These five threads can be resolved into a three-fold theme beginning at the beginning and going right the way through—the Redeemer, the redemption and the redeemed.

To understand the aim of the Bible, we must set that theme against something even greater. We have to take this three-fold theme and put it into the context of God's eternal purpose. It would be quite wrong to say that all the Bible speaks about is this three-fold theme. In fact, we have got to bring it and place it against the backdrop of God's eternal purpose.

Now I have drawn this chart in the hope that perhaps it will help us to understand. I have done it simply, as if this is a library of books, with a rather large volume to begin and a rather large volume to end. And I have put Genesis 1–3 and Revelation 20–22 as the first volume and the last. All these volumes in between are Genesis, Exodus, Leviticus, Numbers, Deuteronomy, Joshua, Judges, and so on, Matthew, Mark, Luke, John, Acts, Romans, and so on. Beginning from before Genesis 1: "In the beginning God," we begin with God's eternal purpose. God had a purpose in the creation of the universe and a purpose in the creation of man, and that purpose was an eternal and spiritual home which outlasts time.

In the first volume, Genesis 1–3, is the original intention of God, and the fall. At the end, we have the original intention realised and the glory which follows. In all these books we have this three-fold theme. It begins in the first three chapters and ends in the last three—Christ appointed as the Redeemer, the cross appointed as the way of redemption, and the redeemed. Of course, the actual, literal work of redemption, was accomplished on the cross, was finished on the cross. However, the work of redemption, the idea of it began in the counsels of God right at the beginning before there ever was a cross. So we have the Redeemer, the redemption, and the redeemed.

The redeemed begin in the first three chapters, but it is a question of whether you believe that Adam and Eve were redeemed. Perhaps you don't. There are some of us who believe that we will see Adam and Eve one day in heaven. Certainly, Abel was saved through the blood of the lamb. Whatever you may feel, the point is this: every

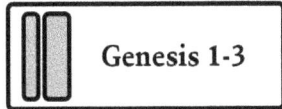

The Redeemer, the Redemption, and the Redeemed

Revelation 20-22

The original intention of God realised

and the glory which follows

Genesis 1-3

The original intention of God

the fall

"In the beginning, God …"

God's purpose before time began

single person who has ever been saved or ever will be saved was in God's heart before ever there was a fall. That is not just Calvinism. Whatever way you look at it, whether you are Arminian or a Calvinist, the point is that in the fore knowledge of God or in the predestination of God's sovereignty, He knew those who were going to be saved. So you have this tremendous three-fold cord running right through from beginning to end. That is the only way you can understand the Bible.

The Bible's Supreme Aim

Let's sum it up: the Bible is a revelation of God's eternal purpose with the supreme aim that we might be saved into it. (We have another chart that may help on the following page.) God's eternal purpose—Christ and His body, the home of God, is the eternal purpose of God.

Here is the creation of man; here are the two trees, the tree of knowledge of good and evil and the tree of life. There are different lines that we have used: solid, short dashes and long dashes. The solid line denotes the eternal purpose of God beginning with the creation of man and running right through to the marriage of the Lamb, the city of God and the ages of the ages. As far as God's eternal purpose is concerned there is no fall. His whole purpose was, whether fall or no fall, that man might become one with Christ in union with Him and go on to marriage with Him and then on to become the city of God, the centre of the administration of the whole universe, heaven and earth, and then the ages of the ages lying dimly behind, as it were, in the far distant future.

Ages
of →
Ages

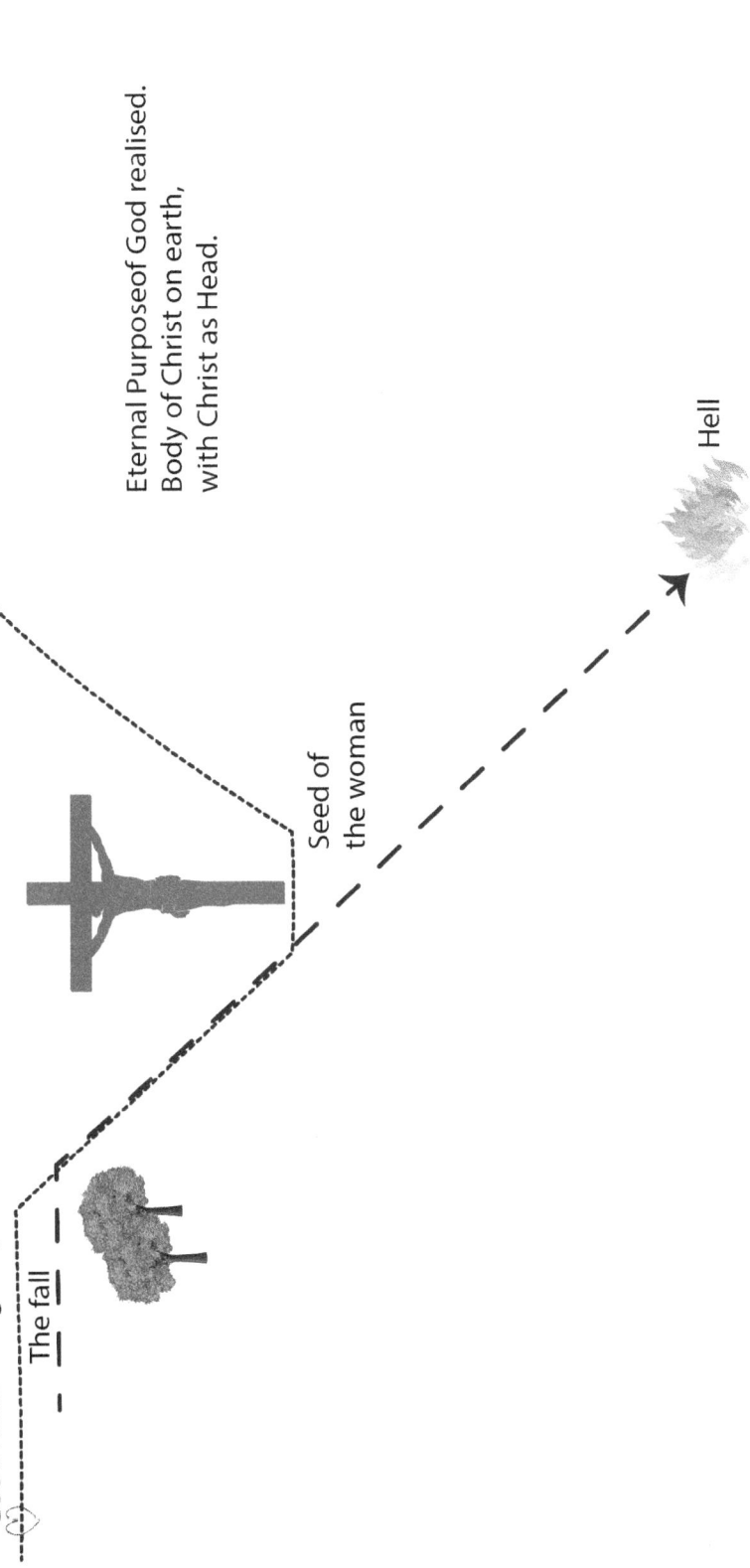

God's Eternal Purpose
God's Redeeming Purpose (from times eternal)

Marraige of the Lamb   City of God

Eternal Purposeof God realised.
Body of Christ on earth,
with Christ as Head.

Hell

Seed of
the woman

The fall

The line with long dashes marks the fall, and you will see it comes down right the way to the cross and then it continues on down to hell. It begins with the tree of the knowledge of good and evil and marks the downward course of mankind, as it fell in the beginning when it took of the tree of the knowledge of good and evil and became a different creature to the one God intended him to be, and thus passed on its constitution to its children and on to their children.

Alongside that line you will see a line with short dashes, and this line marks the redeeming purpose of God. It is closely allied to the eternal purpose of God; for its whole objective by redemption is to bring us back into the eternal purpose of God. It begins in God's heart, as it were, moves on to where the seed of the woman is born and the eternal purpose of God dawns, as it were, in a new way on this fallen earth with Christ as the Head. It should have been up with the solid line, but now it starts down in a fallen and ruined earth.

Then there is the cross and there are two lines—the line of God's eternal purpose and the line of redemption, the so great salvation because of a Lamb slain. It is for every man and woman, who through the lamb slain trusts in Christ in God for forgiveness and cleansing of his sin and for the gift of eternal life, starts on the course which leads to the marriage supper of the Lamb, on into the city of God, and onto the ages of the ages.

I do not know whether that helps you, but you see in a very simple chart form we have tried to illustrate what I have said. The Bible is a revelation of God's eternal purpose with the supreme aim of our being saved into it. We must understand that our salvation is a means to an end. I am not going to take up whether it is possible to be saved and yet still lose one's inheritance in the city of God. That may well be, but the whole point is this: so great salvation is the means by which God takes fallen men and women such as you and me, sinful, unclean as we are, and saves us and puts us back into God's original and eternal purpose.

The scope of the Bible is therefore governed by God's eternal purpose in its immediate and practical application. There is a great deal about God's eternal purpose of which the Bible does not speak. We must say that. I am going to tell you a few of the things just to give you some problem. There are a tremendous number of things that the Bible does not touch on, which it could touch on concerning the eternal purpose of God and the destiny of His people. The whole point is this: the scope of the Bible is governed by God's eternal purpose in its immediate and practical application. Let's just face that. What does that mean? It means that you and I have to be saved. That is the immediate application. If you and I want to get into the eternal purpose of God we have to be saved, and we have to be saved not by our own works, not by our own goodness, but by faith in Christ through the grace of God. That is the only way—through the blood of the Lamb, through the death of Christ. That is the immediate and practical application. However, you do not just know it in your head; you open your heart and take the Lamb as your only basis of salvation. That is the immediate and practical application.

Another immediate and practical application is that you and I have got to become holy people, and that hits hard. In other words, we have to be sanctified. We have to be perfected. It is the only way that we can be brought into God's eternal purpose. The scope of the Bible is all about being saved and then being prepared. It is all about that old man and old nature being dealt with—how it is dealt with, how it is put out of the picture, how the new man is fed and developed, how the new man must grow. It is all a question of living stones. It is not just *a* living stone, but living stones being built together. That is the immediate and practical application of the eternal purpose of God. He wants a home, so it is not just a question of you and I being saved. Once we are saved, we should not only live holy, separate and sanctified lives through the work of the cross and the Holy Spirit, but we should become members of one another in Christ. We should become members of one body. We should become living stones built together into a house, a habitation of God in the spirit. That is the immediate and practical application.

The Bible's Scope—Time

Let's look at this chart at the beginning of the chapter again. What is the scope of the Bible? You can see this open book. It is supposed to be the Bible and its scope. You will see that the scope of the Bible begins just before time and ends just after time. In other words, this middle section is time. The Bible does not say very much about before times eternal, nor does it say a lot about the ages to come. The principle material of the Bible is all to do with the beginning of time to the end of time. That is the principal objective of the Bible and the principle that governs the inclusion of most of its material. It has some things to say about before times eternal, but there are lots of questions we do not have answered.

It says quite a lot about the ages to come, but leaves a tremendous amount unanswered. Sometimes some of us would probably wish there were certain stories that had been left out of the Bible and we had a little bit more about other things. But the whole point of the Bible is to show us what man is and it is faithful in revealing to us the nature of man, even of saved men and women. How easy it is to revert, how easy it is to fall. It is faithful in its record and in touch with life, showing us just what we are made of.

The scope therefore of the Bible is I trust clearly defined in your mind. If you want to have a lot of questions answered about the prehistoric times, I do not think the Bible is going to say much about that. If you want to have a lot of questions answered about the far eternal future, I do not think the Bible is going to say a lot about that. The scope of the Bible is to do with you and me and life as we now live it, why something has gone wrong and how God is moved to put it right, and the way you and I can be in the good of what He has done. Furthermore, if we are in the good of what He has done, we have a hope for the future. We must therefore carefully note that much is mentioned only vaguely and much is left out altogether. In other instances facts are stated without explanation, interpretation, or corroboration. The aim of the Bible governs its scope.

The Bible's Silence Concerning Great Civilisations

Let's look at some of the things the Bible does not even mention. There is not a mention of the great Chinese Empire, nor does it mention the great Indian civilisation, nor the great Inca civilisation. These things are not even touched upon. I know there have been some ingenious scholars who have tried to make some of the rather more unusual names in Isaiah and elsewhere refer to China, and in some cases they have tried to make it refer to India, but on the whole it cannot be proven. As far as China is concerned, it does not seem to be even mentioned in Scripture, and yet one of the greatest, if not the greatest civilisations that the world has ever witnessed, flowered in China. The standard of life and everything else was above any of its contemporaries. It is a remarkable fact that on the whole we have no mention of these civilisations. The Bible passes over them in silence. You may know a little bit about Chinese civilisation and Indian civilisation, but I do not know how much you know about Inca civilisation. However, if you have seen any of the pictures of some of the cities up in the Andes you must be amazed. Whatever are they doing up there? How did they build them? It is the evidence of a most remarkable civilisation, and yet the Bible has nothing to say.

Then again, look at that which the Bible only mentions in a somewhat vague way. It only really mentions it because it touches God's people. Take Egypt. If you look to the Bible to be a kind of handbook on Egyptology, you are going to be upset. It touches on quite a few things in Egyptian civilisation, but it is just here and there. It is the same with Babylon, with Persia, with Greece, and with Rome. All these great civilizations are mentioned, and yet somehow it just states a few facts and leaves us with some very big queries. Why didn't the Bible tell us which pharaoh it was that Joseph labored under? It would have been much simpler if the Bible had just simply told us his name, but it doesn't. It describes certain details of life, details of government and administration, particularly, for instance, in Daniel and elsewhere that have proven to be absolutely accurate. It is one of the most remarkable things in Scripture, but it has just touched on these great civilisations only because they happen to touch God's people.

Let's take Babylon. Scriptures have more to say about Babylon than any other great civilisation. Why? Because Babylon is taken up as a symbol in God's Word of the world, in all of its genius and might. Therefore we have quite a story of Babylon. We are told who founded it and about the tower of Babel which in Scripture is connected with it. Then we go right the way through until we come to Revelation and Babylon is gone. The city is finished long ago, but we still have Babylon. The interesting thing is that John takes it up and talks a lot about Babylon, the great harlot of the nations, because the Scripture is taking it as a symbol.

Then, of course, we have to note what the Bible focuses attention upon. There is a little tiny nation called Israel with no great civilisation, which has left us no great monuments of architecture or anything else, but the whole Bible is focused upon this little people. It tells us details about their life and about God's ways with them. It traces them right back to Abraham and tells us the whole history of that nation from the moment God appeared to Abraham in Ur of the Chaldees and told him to get out from there. Then it traces the whole story of Abraham, Isaac, Jacob, Joseph, and on to Moses, and then a nation. It is a most remarkable thing.

The Bible's Silence Concerning Great Men

Again, may I make mention of a few other things? Have you ever noticed the silence of the Bible about some great men? For instance, do you know the Bible has nothing to say about Confucius? I do not know whether you expect one day to see Confucius in heaven. I do. The Bible has nothing to say about him or Mencius, but in their own day and in their own way these men were tremendous for the purity of their lives and the morality of their teaching. I'm afraid there is a lot of rubbish and nonsense that is taught, sometimes even by missionaries about Confucianism. Maybe it is about what it has come to be, but in its pure form, oh, there is such a lot that is good about the teaching of Confucius.

Take that amazing man called Mo-tzu who comes onto history and passes off and we have so many questions about him. He was a contemporary of Abraham, and one of the most remarkable figures in world history because he taught universal love and he gathered people all over Pakistan, Inner Mongolia, and northwestern China into groups of disciples who practiced love. It has been called the pre-Christian church, yet we have just a little of what he taught and he is gone. He is not mentioned in the Bible.

Go to a man like Lao Tzu and his great document, *The Way of Virtue*. There is so much that is good and it is not mentioned in Scripture. You come to Buddha and you know what Buddha himself taught. I don't think we can always argue with a lot. There was a man who was seeking out for God. And there is Zoroaster, the great Persian. We come to Plato and Aristotle and they are not mentioned in Scripture; it passes over them in absolute silence. Yet Scripture takes a man called Job who is not even one of the Israelites, but a Gentile, and it devotes a large portion of the Old Testament to the story of Job.

The Bible's Inclusion of the Seemingly Insignificant

Think of a little person like Ruth, a Gentile woman, married to a child of God against God's law, and you have a whole book that tells the story of her life. Think of Hannah who was a child of God and yet what has she left us with? If you and I had written history, we would probably never have recorded Hannah's story. We would have perhaps included Confucius or Mencius, or someone else. However, God in His wisdom included the story of Hannah because, in fact, it was one of the great turning points in the history of God's people.

Look at the story of Samson. I know there are some Christians who have felt that the story of Samson could well have been left out of the Bible. It seems to be a rather sordid story, one that speaks mostly of failure and I am sure that if you and I were compiling the Bible we would have felt there were some other things much better included than the story of Samson. Yet, here we have the story of Samson and these others are overlooked.

Sometimes it would seem that the humanly insignificant is lit up at the expense of what we would call the important. For instance, Rahab; she was a harlot and yet we have a whole story of Rahab. She was the mother of Boaz who married Ruth. Isn't that amazing? Why do you think Rahab was brought into the story? Turn to Matthew chapter 1 and you have the answer. She is in the Messianic line.

Consider Bathsheba. In writing the story of the history of things, don't you think you and I would have left Bathsheba out? We would not have known that Bathsheba was destined to become one in the royal line of the Messiah. You and I would not have thought it. Perhaps we would have felt that rather heavy story, that unhappy episode in David's life was best left out. Perhaps you would have said, "It is insignificant. It is sordid. It is evil and insignificant in light of the tremendous things of David's reign." Yet, God's Holy Spirit brings it into the record, because another thousand years on, Jesus Christ was to be born to Joseph and Mary, and Bathsheba was in the Messianic line.

Then there is the Song of Solomon, an amazing story. What is it to do with? We do not really know. Humanly speaking, was it a story of his love for his queen or his love for someone else in his large number of wives? What is this story? Do you think you and I would have actually included it? Do you think there were some other documents we may have felt would have been better? Yet, the Holy Spirit includes the Song of Solomon because it is the greatest allegory in the whole of Scripture of the love of God for His church. At the time we would never have thought of it, but she is covered.

What about the little book of Haggai and its building programme? Do you think really that little book of two chapters is worth its place in the Scripture? Do you think you might have felt at the time: Now it is all over. Surely that is one of the little documents that could fall out after all. This temple that we have built is really not very marvellous. Look at the pyramids in Egypt. Look at some of the other great temples. Look at some of the great structures that have gone up. What is this little temple in Jerusalem, really? It is only bricks and mortar and God will think of something greater than that perhaps if we had more spiritual insight or perception. Nevertheless, God in His wisdom has kept the little book of Haggai in Scripture because although it may seem insignificant it has a tremendous lesson for us.

The point is that most of the ordinary historical and biographical narratives in Scripture, in so far as it records facts, could have been written by any contemporary historian or biographer. However, in the Bible it is interpreted in the light of God's purpose and redemption, and that is the difference. History takes on a new light because it is placed into the whole setting of God's eternal purpose and His redeeming work, both biography and history.

Unanswered Questions

Now, there are many questions that are either not answered at all or only partially answered. I am just going to give you a few. What is the origin of sin? Where did it come from? Oh, someone says, "I know that; the Bible tells us—Satan." Yes, but how did it first appear in Satan? That is not answered in Scripture.

Let me ask you another question. Was there a pre-Adamic race? In other words, was there a race of men before Adam? We do not know. There are some amazing inferences in God's Word, but that is all. The question is not answered. There are some who would like to believe it and indeed did teach it, but was there another race?

Does the Bible tell us whether there are any other planets inhabited by man or men? For instance, I once heard one great, well-known, evangelical preacher speak on the ninety and nine. He told us that all the other planets, which were inhabited, have never fallen and have gone on into God's great purpose, but that we were the black sheep, this planet, this universe and had strayed off. Is this silly? There are universes upon universes upon universes. Is there somewhere else, some others that are inhabited? Have they been tempted and touched with sin? The Bible does not tell us anything about that.

How does God's sovereignty and man's free will tie up? That is another one, but the Bible does not really answer that. It only states the fact on both sides and leaves it. How does it tie up? Tell me, in what measure is God directly sovereign in the affairs of nations? Here again the Bible states facts. It would seem as if God actually takes full charge in some cases, and in others He leaves them. Here again, the Bible does not actually answer it. Oh, there are many questions that we have!

Do you think the Bible tells us what we shall do in heaven? Of course, it does tell us that we shall sing; but is that all we shall do in heaven? Tell me, does the Bible say anything about clothes, food, or habits? I could ask you a number of questions about the life to come, about which the Bible has nothing to say. Of course, one that we often hear asked is: "Shall we recognise each other in heaven?" When the Lord Jesus was raised from the dead, He was evidently clothed. Think that one out. He ate royal fish, but it does not mean anything. These are things that are mysteries. You can smile at them, but when you go away and think about them, there is something in them.

I will ask another question which may seem a little amusing. What about people's idiosyncrasies? It is all very well to say we will not have those in heaven, but you know, half a person's character is gone when they have lost some of those little oddities. But do we have to put up with them in heaven or not? Those little oddities in people's characters are in fact part of a person, but the Bible has nothing to say about them.

Again, does the Bible say anything about what exactly happened to the natural creation? According to the Bible when the natural creation was first created, it did not feed on meat, and yet, and yet, and yet, what happened and when did it happen? The whole creation was vegetarian in the beginning. What happened and how did the constitution of the creation change? These are questions, many questions.

There are many other questions too, perhaps not as big as those, but as important. For instance, what did Christ do between the years of twelve and thirty? I know that He was a carpenter, but wouldn't you love to know a little bit about His life, of the difficulties He must have had in the carpenter's shop, the difficult customers, the long hours of work? We should like to know a lot more about that. What was Christ like as a child?

What did Moses do in his first eighty years? We know a little bit about it; but there are some marvellous traditions in the Talmud about Moses. They say that he was one of the greatest heroes in Egypt because he led the campaign against Libya. Is it true or not true? It is said that he forsook wealth, that he turned his back on all the greatness and wealth of Egypt, preferring to cast in his lot with the people of God. That is the only inference we have in Scripture that he left something very great. Wouldn't it be wonderful if we knew? But the Bible does not say. God knows best and He has not told us. What did Moses do for forty years looking after sheep? Of course, we know he was looking after sheep, but I would like to know a good deal more about his life there.

I have often wondered: did Hosea's marriage work out in the end? After all that marvellous story in the book of Hosea, when he finally went and rebought her after more trouble, did it work out in the finish? Did they live happily together?

How did Jeremiah write Lamentations in acrostic form and in *qinah* rhythm which is like the funeral dirge[1]? How did Jeremiah write Lamentations, which is the most moving and remarkable of the documents amongst the prophets? How did he write it with each verse beginning with A, then B, and so on, and in *qinah* rhythm? We are not told.

Who wrote the Hebrew letter? Many say Paul wrote it, but it does not say Paul. There is a great discussion as to who it was. Was it Apollos? Was it Paul? Was it Timothy? Who wrote the Hebrew letter? It would be very interesting, but we are not told.

Did Paul make a mistake in going to Jerusalem? Remember the prophet came and bound his hands and said, "The Holy Spirit says if you go to Jerusalem you will have bonds"? The church prayed and said to him: "Do not go up, Paul. We are sure you are going to make a mistake." Paul went, and what happened? He got into trouble and, as we know, he got a free ticket to Rome as a prisoner. He had always purposed to go to Rome, but did he make a mistake? Scripture does not say.

Was Paul married? If he was, what happened to his wife? It would solve a lot of people's queries and suppositions and speculations if they could only know whether Paul in fact was married. So you have all these different questions.

These and many more are left unanswered in so far as they are not important to our understanding of the Bible's aim. In fact not one of those questions is really important to our understanding

---

1 3 stress stichos, followed by 2-stress—3:2

of the Bible's aim in its immediate and practical application. The wonder of it is that whenever it touches the immediate and practical application, the Bible is absolutely clear and dogmatic.

The Revelation of God's Eternal Purpose

We see that the Bible is a revelation of God's eternal purpose with the aim of our being awakened, saved and incorporated. There are just a few things we could mention which may help.

God's Sovereign Working

We have talked quite a lot about God's eternal purpose, and now we see within the pages of the Bible, an omnipotent God working according to the counsel of His own will and sovereignly performing His purpose. You may have an argument about that, but it does not bother me. The point is that Scripture declares right the way through from beginning to end that it is an omnipotent God that rules. An omnipotent God is working everything out, even in this fallen world with all its strife and trouble, according to the counsel of His own will. He is sovereignly performing His own purpose all in due time. That is the first thing.

God's Son as Head and Heir

Here is the second thing, and this is wonderful. The Bible reveals within its pages His original and eternal purpose that His Son should be Head of all things and Heir of all things. It reveals that a people originally meant to be mankind in union with Him, part of Him, should share that with Him. That is the second thing.

God's Determination to Save a People

The third thing we find within the pages of the Bible is this: the foreseeing by God of the fall and the ruin of man and the determination of God to save a people out of a fallen mankind. In them and through them He will secure His original intention still to make Christ Head and Heir over all things with a people joined to Him.

As an aside, when man ate of the tree of the knowledge of good and evil, he chose to become head over all things himself and heir to all things himself. That is exactly the story of fallen mankind. They have become the ruler of it all—they think. In fact, the lie of the whole thing is that Satan himself has become head over all. He is prince of the powers of the air, prince of this world; he has become head over it all and hopes to be heir of it all. That is why there is a battle, because Satan has said, "I will be like the Most High; I will exalt my throne to the throne of God." So this great battle commenced as to who is going to be head and heir of all things, and man is the key because Satan has got hold of man as a vessel in which he indwells. He is in it! Sometimes you can see Satan, and we know it ourselves, don't we? We can see it in our old nature sometimes that he is there; something that comes out of the pit. He is there in us. It only has to be played upon and out it comes. On the other hand, God's purpose is that the Son should be Head and Heir, and that He should have a people in whom He dwells, who is goodness and purity and righteousness itself. So that is the third thing.

The Ministry of God's Son

The fourth thing is this and I love this. The Bible reveals in its pages the appointment of the Son, from the beginning to a saving, keeping and perfecting ministry, and His appearance in due time in this world amongst men to live, to die, and to be raised is the basis of His ministry. I love that because it just means that the Lord Jesus was not an afterthought; God appointed Him from the beginning to a saving ministry. Isn't that wonderful! The Lord Jesus now is alive at the right hand of God the Father. What is He doing? His basis is that He lived a perfect life, He died a complete death, and He was raised as the evidence that God had accepted it. He is at the right hand of God on that basis of shed blood and a broken body, ever living to make intercession. He can save to the uttermost them that come unto God by Him seeing that He ever lives to make intercession.

He is there at the right hand of God in a saving ministry. Listen! If you call upon the name of the Lord Jesus right now and the Lord Jesus says to the Father, "Save him! Save her! I died for that one." That is His saving ministry. Not only that, it is a keeping ministry. If you and I get into trouble, we only have to look up to Jesus and He says to the Father, "Keep him. Keep her." There is His perfecting ministry. There is One watching over us, and in everything He is seeking to perfect what is of Himself, get rid of the dross, and refine what is of Himself.

The Holy Spirit's Calling

Fifthly, there is the calling out by the Holy Spirit of a people from every nation to be the body of Christ. Of course this is revealed within the pages of God's Word. What is happening today? Everywhere, in nearly every nation, if not every nation under the sun, there is a great work going on of the Holy Spirit. It may seem in some places to be very insignificant, but it is the clarion call of the Gospel of God. Out of every nation and tongue and kindred and people there are coming those who are washing themselves in the blood of the Lamb and are becoming the family of God. This is the great work of the Holy Spirit sent forth on the day of Pentecost to call out a people to be the bride and the body of God's Son.

God's Final Vindication and Triumph

Sixthly, the Bible reveals within its pages the final vindication and triumph of God and His purpose fulfilled. This is I believe a great help. There are people who sneer at prophecy. They feel that somehow or other it just can't be because somehow it is so supernatural, it is outside the realm of human intelligence, and it baffles. We have the capacity sometimes of just trying to turn away from it just because it is so remarkable, but prophecy is a fact. God knew that His people were going to have a long drawn-out battle, in which at times the enemy would seem to be violently on top, so He allowed the prophets to prophesy of all that would come to pass.

You may think it strange, but in the days at the end of this age, whether it is a hundred years, two hundred years, or farther off, some Scriptures are going to be more precious to God's children than anything else. It will be parts of the book of Revelation, parts of Matthew 24, and parts of Daniel. Why? Because they foretold centuries and centuries and centuries ago that the end would see the reign of the antichrist, Satan incarnate. When the Christians are literally being persecuted to the death everywhere, as it says in Scripture, if those days were not shortened it were not possible that the elect themselves would be saved. It says that the dragon went to pursue the seed of the woman to destroy it from off the face of the earth. When those days come, there will be this in the Scripture that makes people in all their persecution and martyrdom look up and realise that God is on the throne. Why? Because He foresaw it all and foretold it all and revealed the ultimate triumph.

When Jesus went to the cross, it would have been easy for Him if thousands upon thousands of angels had gathered around, and as He died on that cross He could have seen the triumph that was to be His. He did not see it. All He saw was blackness and all He felt was forsakenness, but He knew that it had been foretold that this was the work of redemption and that when He died, God would raise Him up again.

So it will be in the end when the church is in its last great phases before the return of the Lord. It will seem as if it is lost and forsaken and the night has come when no man can work. That will be a day when no man can work, and in that day, oh how glad we shall be for the pages of this Book, which will be revealed in absolute and final vindication of God and the fulfillment of His purpose. We have been saved through the cross, and we are no longer on the path that Jesus called the broad way that leads to destruction. We are in the narrow way that leads to eternal life. Oh, that you and I might press on, really press on, to know the Lord more and more fully!

"Wise Unto Salvation"

I think that we must note carefully that the Bible according to its own word is able to make us wise unto salvation. Isn't that a wonderful word in II Timothy 3:15: "And that from a babe thou hast known the sacred writings which are able to make thee wise unto salvation through faith which is in Christ Jesus"? *Wise unto salvation.*

What is the aim of this Book? To make us wise unto salvation. Do not despise it. Do not degrade it. Do not dishonour it. Do not give it a place any lower than the place Christ gave to it. This Book, these sacred writings are able to make you wise unto salvation through faith; not through unbelief, but through faith in Christ Jesus. You can have this Book in your hand and be blind to salvation; you can have this Book in your hand and be wise unto salvation. Why? The key is faith. If you need to be delivered, if you need to know something more of your so great salvation, if you need to know it more deeply, more fully, it is faith that is the key. If you come to this Book with unbelief it will not speak to you. It will only mock you. But if you come to it with faith, it will make you wise to something more in your so great salvation.

"To Make Us Complete"

But it does more than that. It is able to make us complete, as the Revised Standard Version puts it, "...to make us complete, equipped to every good work." The word complete is a lovely word. It means "fitted out, furnished," as the old Authorised Version puts it, "thoroughly furnished." It is the idea of a house which is empty and you begin to put the curtains up and the lampshades on. The carpet is put down, the furniture is put in, and it is thoroughly furnished. It is equipped. You can have a kitchen, and all you have is four walls, a floor, a ceiling and a tap. It is not much of a kitchen. It has got to be complete and equipped to every good work. You need the pots and pans, you need a cooker, you need all the utensils, and then you need the food. You have got to have everything so it is thoroughly furnished. This is the word.

What is the aim of the Bible? It is to make you wise unto salvation, yes, in an initial way, and in an ever greater way through faith. However, it is to do more. It is to fit you out unto every good work. In other words, it is to put into your experience, into your hand every single thing you need to live a godly life full of good works. That is this Book. Do you need to be saved? This is the Book. Do you need to be sanctified? This is the Book. Do you need to be kept? This is the Book.

Do you know what has been coming to me recently? "Thy word have I hidden in my heart that I might not sin against Thee" (Psalm 119:11). "How can a young man cleanse his way? By taking heed according to your word" (Psalm 119:9). Jesus said, "You are clean because of the word that I have spoken to you" (John 15:3). Again it is the Book. What a lot is within its covers! The Bible therefore has not merely the aim of our being saved and incorporated into God's purpose, but the power in the hand of the Holy Spirit to do it, which is the most important thing of all. It has the power to do it, but there is one thing required—faith. It says in Hebrews chapters 3 and 4, that those whose hearts were mixed with unbelief fell when they received the word of God, because as they heard the Word of God they said, "It cannot be! Not me, not me! It cannot be! It is not for me." But faith like a grain of mustard seed takes hold of God's Word and says, "That's it! That is true if every man proves to be a liar." There was a time when I thought myself bigger than God's Word and tended to look down upon it a little and question it in all kinds of ways. But then there came a time when I came to this simple position that God's Word is true even if I am a liar, and if every other man proves to be a liar. Since then I have discovered that God's Word works. When there is an attitude of real faith to God's Word, it works.

The Book of Unchanging Principles

We ought finally to mention that the Bible is a Book of unchanging principles, and once we are saved it is a matter of spiritual education in those principles. Now, I do not mean regulations and I do not mean laws. I mean principles, things that are inherent within the life of God, and the Bible shows them. We read in Hebrews 4:12 how the Word of God is sharper than any two-edged sword living, active and able to cut and do the work if we will only let it. So there you are. They are the first rudiments of the Word of God, and we ought to go on from milk to solid food so that we grow.

How do we grow? It is by using our spiritual facilities, and as we use our spiritual facilities so we grow up. What we receive we must use, and what we receive we must put into practice. Those principles are vital to our spiritual health and growth. We could say a lot about principles, but I think that is your job to find out those principles that are within God's Word. They are there, and many of those stories in the Old Testament and through the ages were written to reveal principles, for instance, faith. It underlies everything from beginning to end. "The righteous or the just shall live on the principle of faith" (see Romans 1:17; Galatians 3:11; Hebrews 10:38). Once you move off the principle of faith everything stops.

Let's take the principle of the cross. If you assert yourself, if you start saying "I" you begin to sort of die spiritually. You are finished spiritually. It is the old law of the flesh in operation. But if you learn the principle of the cross—what it is to die, to let go, and just trust in Him—you find a new principle of life, the principle of risen life, of resurrection.

There is the principle of travail. What is the principle of travail? There is nothing of real value without suffering. It is behind everything. If you look right through the whole of this Book, you will find this principle wherever you look. Everything that means something to God comes through travail.

There is the principle of separation. Wherever there is mixture there is unhappiness. There is no greater truth. Wherever there is mixture there is unhappiness, and God's Word is filled with examples of this simple principle. Where there is purity of heart and purity of hand, there is joy. But where sin has come in, or worldliness and it has corrupted, tainted and spoiled, there is unhappiness, emptiness, and a vacuum. Of course, the enemy's whole job is to rob Christians of what is theirs, rob them of their life. Here they are as witnesses. Witnesses to what? To eternal life, but they are not enjoying it. They are witnesses to joy, but they do not have any joy. They are full of moans and aches and groans. Witnesses to salvation, but it does not seem to work. They have a salvation that they sing about and pray about, but it is not in practical operation. They are not *being* saved.

The aim of the Bible is that you and I may be awakened, saved, and incorporated into the eternal purpose of God. That is the supreme aim of the Bible. How? By the Redeemer, and by His redeeming work. That is how. The scope of the Bible is the immediate and practical application of that great purpose of God as far as you and I go individually and corporately.

6.
The Structure and Growth of the Bible

Where does the word Bible come from? I think you understand that this word Bible is not found within the Scriptures themselves. Where, in fact, do we get this word? The word Bible came through Latin from the Greek biblia, and it was plural. Originally, Greek-speaking Christians called the Scriptures "The Books" because of the number of books that make up the Scriptures. Ancient books were written on papyrus or what the Greeks called byblos, imported from Egypt through a town which came to be called Byblos. They began to write upon a split reed of a plant that grows in Egypt which was made into some kind of parchment type of paper, and as a result the Greeks used to call any written document or book a Biblion. From that word, the plural Biblia, the Scriptures, the Bible came to receive this title. They were called not the book but the books. When the Greek word for the Scriptures passed into Latin, it was treated as a singular noun. It was taken straight over from Greek and just simply treated as singular and came to be called "The

Book." From that it passed into English and many other languages more or less in the same way and became the Bible. That is how we came to have this title "The Bible."

The Bible is, in fact, both one book and at the same time a library of sixty-six books in all. For the most part these sixty-six books are quite distinct, although there were some that were bound together originally as one book. For instance, I and II Kings were, in fact, one book originally, and also I and II Samuel were originally one book. Ezra and Nehemiah were one volume originally. It is also possible that I and II Chronicles, a two-fold work and one book originally, were bound with Ezra and Nehemiah and made all one volume originally. We know that Ezra and Nehemiah were one but we are not absolutely certain that Chronicles was added in with them. It is also possible that Judges and Ruth were originally one volume because there is a certain amount of evidence to suggest it. Of course, I think you all know that Luke and Acts were two parts of one work. Originally, when they were first written, they were bound together and were, in fact, a history of Christian origins in two parts—the first, Christ, as it were, and second, the church. We have often said that Luke could have well entitled his work, "The New Man" the first part, "The Head, the Lord Jesus Christ," and the second part, "The Body of the Lord Jesus Christ, the Church." But originally these were one volume.

Nevertheless, for the most part, the sixty-six books which we now have and comprise this library that we call "The Bible" are distinctive. They cover a period during which they were written of not less than one thousand-five hundred years, the New Testament being confined to the last hundred years approximately of that whole time. The books were written over quite a large area, ranging from Italy in the west to Mesopotamia in the East, possibly as far East as Persia. There were all these different places that parts of the Scriptures were written, covering quite a large area.

The Diversity of the Bible Writers

The writers were not only parted by time and parted by locality or place, but they were greatly diverse in their background. There are writers who were kings, others who were priests, others who were prophets. There are some noblemen and courtiers, shepherds, peasants, and fishermen. We even have a fig tree dresser. That was a gentleman who went up into the tree before it ripened and had to puncture each of the sycamore figs in order to help it to really ripen. There are statesmen, soldiers, and we have at least one doctor of medicine, Dr. Luke. There is at least one doctor of law, Dr. Paul, and at least one ex-tax collector, Matthew. So the writers of this Book really have a most remarkably diverse background. Of course, there are a number of others that you probably can think of, but I have just simply noted down those that came to me.

Then we find that every kind of literary method is employed in this library of books. We have everything from biography, personal memoirs and personal diaries (there are diaries included in Scripture), from personal correspondence to more general correspondence. We have not only all that but there is poetry, there are parables, allegory, and then on to prophecy and clear, dogmatic teaching.

The Harmony and Unity of the Sixty-six Books

The whole range of literary method is found in this library. It is truly a library, and yet with all its diversity there is a unity from its beginning to its end. True, it is not the apparent technical unity of a machine; it is rather the living unity of a plant or an organism. It is not quite so apparent, yet its unity is expressed in many different ways. Once you really look into it you discover there is this amazing unity, which gives the whole of this library harmony and cohesion. There is no human editor, no one human compiler, there is no one human anthologist, there is no editorial committee; yet somehow over the centuries of time it has grown until it has reached what we now know as "The Bible." Its unity has sprung from within instead of being applied from without. Thus, in one sense, it is an almost unconscious unity. The writers were not conscious of harmonizing what they said with those who went before and certainly not those who were going to come after them. It was an unconscious unity. They must have known, of course, in speaking of certain things that they were holding to what had already been revealed, and possibly developing certain thoughts, certain aspects of what God had revealed. Nevertheless, it was an unconscious unity, which gradually developed over the centuries until we have what we now call "The Bible." This unity is a wonderful thing just because it is so unconscious; for it is hidden in many ways behind tremendous diversity and variation in every way. I do believe that unless our hearts are really enlightened and the Holy Spirit is leading us, we fail to see that unity and can sometimes only be taken up with the diversity and with the variation of detail.

These sixty-six books are divided into two unequal halves. I hope you will forgive me for being so utterly simple, but I am starting absolutely from scratch just as if no one knows what the Bible is. The sixty-six books are divided into two unequal halves—thirty-nine books in the first division, which we commonly call the Old Testament and twenty-seven in the second division, which is commonly called the New Testament.

The first thing I want to do is to look at the whole matter of the Old and the New Testaments. This is the first great division in the structure of the Bible. The sixty-six books are a library, and yet a unity. That is the first thing. The second thing is that it is divided into two unequal parts—one section of thirty-nine books, the other section of twenty-seven books, which we now call the Old and New Testaments.

The Origin of the Name "Testament"

The word testament came to be used of this major two-fold division of the Bible due to a mistranslation of a Greek word, which meant firstly "arrangement," or "disposition," or "testament," or "will" in the sense of "last testament and will." That is what it first meant, and it had a second meaning of "covenant" or "pact." In the Septuagint Version, which is the oldest translation of the Old Testament into Greek, this Greek word was used to translate the Hebrew word used so much as "covenant." It was understood clearly by all readers of the Greek version of the Old Testament to mean "covenant." It is interesting actually to note that there was another Greek word which could have been translated and used for the Hebrew word covenant and could have done the job very well.

However, it is noteworthy that the Septuagint translators rejected it out of hand because that particular word had the idea within it of a pact or agreement between equals, and they had sufficient spiritual understanding of God's Word to recognize that the Hebrew word covenant did not mean a pact between two equals. This is very, very important. I think many of us have this idea that covenant means a kind of mutual pact. In fact the Biblical idea of covenant means God's pact or God's settlement or God's covenant freely made by Him in sovereign grace. That is, it is God who initiates the covenant, and it is God who gives it freely to us. I think that has to be understood very clearly at the outset.

The Septuagint translators felt that the first Greek word we have spoken of was better suited to this Biblical, Hebrew conception of the word covenant than the second. The Septuagint Version differs quite considerably in some ways from our Hebrew Version of the Old Testament. When the Septuagint Version was translated from Greek into Latin, we get the Latin Vulgate which, of course, originally was the Bible of Western Europe. Our own English Bible originally stemmed from this Latin Vulgate. When this translation was made from the Greek into the Latin, two words vied for the honour of translating this Greek word covenant. One word was testamental and the second was instrumental. The first word was favoured very greatly by all European scholars, and the second word was favoured very greatly by all the North African scholars. Over quite a long period of time, there was a great division of opinion as to which Latin word should be used to translate this Greek word that the Septuagint translators had used for the Hebrew word covenant.

Now this first word, testamental, meant "testament" or "will" or "arrangement"; instrumental, interestingly enough meant a "legally binding agreement or document." In many ways, it is very interesting to follow the whole course of this. I do not think we can completely follow it because it would take far too much time and it is far too involved to explain it simply enough. The trouble all stemmed from a misunderstanding by the Latin translators of the Greek Septuagint, the Greek version, as to this Greek word. Whereas the Greek translators understood it to mean "covenant," the Latin translators took it to mean "will" or "testament" or "arrangement." Finally, it was the European side that won and testamental was universally used for the word covenant, and thus it passed into English as the word testament. So we have our word the Old Testament and the New Testament.

It would have been very interesting if the word instrumental had won the day, for then we would possibly have had the Old Instrument and the New Instrument. In many ways we would have been nearer to the idea of this two-fold division of the Bible—the first instrument God used to bring His people to His salvation and the second instrument that He used. This is the history of it, the explanation, the expression of it contained in these books. It would have been very interesting if in fact that word had won the day. It would probably have been nearer to the original idea of a binding agreement or document which God had made. It did not, and in the end, this word testamental came in and passed into English as testament.

The Old and New Covenant

The use of the word testament is in many ways quite misleading. Most people, if they understand it at all, do not understand it as the books expressing the Old Covenant and those expressing the New Covenant, but rather as a last will and testament. How do you look upon the Old Testament? Why are the first thirty-nine books of the Bible called the Old Testament? Have you ever thought why the word testament is used? What does it mean? There are very few Christians who associate that word testament with covenant and the whole point is it should have been covenant. Indeed some of the revised versions have gone back to that now and have put the Old Covenant and the New Covenant. However, in the newest version they have gone back again to testament because it is so widely used by everyone, even if wrongly. I suppose it is hard to overcome.

Do you understand that it has nothing to do with the Lord dying and leaving His last will and testament? It is not that the Lord sort of left this to us when He died. This was the written record that He left behind; that is how I used to think of it. No, not at all. It is the books which express and contain the history of the Old Covenant and the books which express and contain the history of the New Covenant. It is as simple as that.

It is important for us to understand this word covenant since it is used to cover the whole Bible. The whole Bible is comprehended by this word covenant whether old or new. What really does it mean? It is unfortunate that in our Authorized Version the word covenant appears in nearly all instances in the Old Testament as "covenant" and in nearly all instances in the New Testament as "testament." Consequently, in the Authorized Version the whole continuity is obscured so that it is very hard to really follow through just what is meant by this word covenant. Now the Revised Version and most all of the modern versions that I can recall, have translated it uniformly as covenant. Let's take our Bibles and look up a number of these references.

Genesis 9:9: "Behold, I establish my covenant with you and your descendants after you." Verse 16: "When the bow is in the clouds, I will look upon it and remember the everlasting covenant between God and every living creature of all flesh that is upon the earth." (the word covenant)

Genesis 15:8: "But Abraham said, "O Lord God, how am I to know that I shall possess it?" He said to him, "Bring me a heifer three years old, a she-goat three years old, a ram three years old, a turtledove and a young pigeon. And he brought Him all these, cut them in two and laid each half over against the other, but he did not cut the birds in two."

Verse 17: "When the sun had gone down and it was dark, behold a smoking fire pot and a flaming torch passed between these pieces. On that day the Lord made a covenant with Abram saying, 'To your descendants I give this land, from the river of Egypt to the great river, the river Euphrates, the land of the Kenites, the Kenizzites, the Kadmonites, the Hittites, the Perizzites, the Rephaim, the Amorites, the Canannites, and the Girgashites, and the Jebusites."

Exodus 24:3, 6–8: "Moses came and told the people all the words of the Lord and all the ordinances; and all the people answered with one voice, and said, 'All the words which the Lord has spoken we will do.'" ... "Moses took half of the blood and put it in basins, and half of the blood he threw against the altar. Then he took the book of the covenant and read it in the hearing of the people, and they said, 'All that the Lord has spoken we will do and we will be obedient.' And Moses took the blood and threw it upon the people, and said, 'Behold, the blood of the covenant which the Lord has made with you in accordance with all these words.'"

There are many, many other instances of the word covenant, but those are three absolutely fundamental references to this word covenant in the Old Testament. And they are sufficient to understand the Old Covenant that God made with His people before Calvary, before the appearance of Christ.

The Lord has intimated in a number of places that the other covenant is only a preparatory one, and here is the first clear dogmatic reference to a new covenant.

Jeremiah 31:31–34: "Behold, the days are coming, says the Lord, when I will make a new covenant for the house of Israel and the house of Judah, not like the covenant which I made with their fathers when I took them by the hand to bring them out of the land of Egypt, my covenant which they broke, though I was their husband, says the Lord. But this is the covenant which I will make with the house of Israel after those days, says the Lord. I will put my law within them, I will write it upon their heart, I will be their God and they shall be my people, and no longer shall each man teach his neighbor and each his brother saying, Know the Lord, for they shall all know me from the least of them to the greatest, says the Lord, for I will forgive their iniquity and I will remember their sin no more." What a wonderful reference that is!

In Matthew 26:28 we have the New Covenant of which Jeremiah spoke and Moses really symbolized in his act when he threw the blood upon the people.

"For this is my blood of the covenant, said the Lord Jesus, which is poured out from heaven for the forgiveness of sin." "This is my blood of the New Covenant."

I Corinthians 11:25: "In the same way also," said Paul, "he took the cup after supper saying, This cup is the new covenant in my blood."

II Corinthians 3:6: "Who has qualified us to be ministers of a new covenant, not in a written code but in the Spirit, for the written code kills but the Spirit gives life."

Hebrews 7:22: "This makes Jesus the surety of a better covenant."

The Biblical Meaning of Covenant

What is the biblical meaning of this word covenant? It means a solemn pact or agreement or settlement initiated by God in His love and grace and mercy. It has been freely bestowed upon us and given to us, ratified by the shedding of precious blood and the death of an innocent victim. It does not matter where you turn in the Bible, this whole library of sixty-six books, you will not find the word covenant alters from that. There was a teaching at one time which tried to make everything in the Old Testament sort of truth and righteousness; it was all law, and everything in the New Testament was grace. While there is an aspect of truth in this, we have to be very careful that we do not take it too far. The word covenant has never altered; it has always meant a solemn pact that has been initiated by God with His own people and has been ratified by the shedding of precious blood and the death of an innocent victim. The whole thing was but a preparation. It was but a symbol, it was but a type of that which was to come. The eternal covenant is a solemn agreement or settlement, a pact initiated by God through Christ with us who are redeemed through faith in Him and ratified by the shedding of Christ's own precious blood and His death on the cross as an absolutely sinless One. That is the covenant that you and I have been brought into by God. Oh, dear child of God, you have not entered into it by your will; God has drawn you into it by His will. It is as solemn and wonderful and as marvellous as that. God has drawn us into this tremendous pact that He has made with us on the one ground of faith. That is simply tremendous!

We sing so often of covenant love, of covenant grace, of covenant mercy, and this word of course is the word in the Old Testament which our translators had the greatest difficulty in translating. Sometimes it is loving kindness; in the Authorized Version it is that beautiful word mercy. In the Revised Version it is lovingkindness and in the Revised Standard Version, steadfast love, but the idea is covenant faithfulness, covenant love. This is God's kind of love, a special kind of love—covenant love, covenant grace, covenant mercy including all these ideas within it. By this covenant God promises to save us, to redeem us, to forgive us, to change us, to glorify us, to give us an eternal inheritance and to share His own life and nature and gifts with us. Now, there could be nothing more marvellous than the covenant that God has made. Once you see that, this word testament pales into insignificance—the Old Covenant and the New Covenant. How wonderful it is—thirty-nine books all to do with the Old Covenant and twenty-seven books all to do with the New Covenant. I say it is tremendous!

This covenant has the sense within it of mutual belonging. Now this is where once we understand that it is God who initiates it through sovereign grace, we get this other idea of something mutual. God gives Himself, and you and I have to give ourselves. God gives Himself through the death of Christ, and you and I have got to give ourselves to God through the death of Christ. In other words, it was Christ who died for us to save us, now we must see that Christ died as us that we might come into union with God. I am not going to take that any further, but it is mutual belonging and this is the basis of the covenant. Once God has saved us, He says, "I give Myself to you; you give yourself to Me. I give Myself to you unreservedly. I do not want your old nature, I do not want your old life, I do not want your old man; I want the whole to go away with Christ into death. I want you alive in Christ. That is what I want, mutual belonging." It is in fact a marriage bond or relationship. The Lord said about the Old Covenant: "Though I was their husband ..." The idea behind covenant is that you and I have been wedded to the Lord, and that is why adultery in Scripture has such somber and solemn overtones because it is a denial and profaning of this covenant relationship.

Then again, covenant has this idea that we call "the covenant circle." This is what the old Presbyterians always called it. It was also mentioned in the revival of Presbyterianism, "the covenant circle." It really means incorporation into God's family and household. Of course, I am afraid some people try to apply it to infants and somehow or other make baptism to speak of this incorporation into the covenant circle. Well, maybe babes of believing parents are incorporated into the covenant circle, but I do not see why we have to add water to it. However, that's by the way.

The point is that covenant stands for incorporation into God's family and household. We are the redeemed of the Lord, and by that redemption we have been placed into God's family and household. He has made a covenant with us and we are His own family. "I shall be their God and they shall be My children." We are a family and we are His household built upon the foundation of the apostles and prophets, Christ Jesus Himself being the chief cornerstone.

The first thirty-nine books of this library are all to do with the old and preparatory covenant, and they illustrate and explain God's ways with His own before the appearance of Christ on the earth. They lead up to and point to the new and eternal covenant, which is expressed and explained in the last twenty-seven books. I do hope I have myself clear.

There were a number of covenants, but we will call it the Old Covenant and cover them all. They are all looking forward to the great new and eternal covenant of the Lord, and the wonderful chapter in Hebrews, which tells us that this New Covenant has made the old obsolete. It has taken over, it has transcended, surpassed them; they were the shadow, this is the substance. Now of course having said that many will surely ask, "Do we really need the Old Covenant? Do we need the thirty-nine books of the Old Covenant now that we have the new? Are they not made obsolete, rendered completely obsolete by the New Covenant?"

We have to remember that the whole Old Testament is a vital preparation and foundation for the New Testament. The Bible of the Lord Jesus and of the apostles and of the early church was literally and exclusively the Old Testament. The thirty-nine books of the Old Covenant and all that we have in the New, flowered and fruited on the bush of the Old.

Some of you have heard these little old jingles, but they are helpful. The New is in the Old contained; the Old is in the New explained. Another one, the New is in the Old concealed; the Old is in the New revealed. You were taught these when you were children. The New is in the Old enfolded; the Old is in the New unfolded. These are very simple little jingles, but they help. They get into the heart and in the end they often lead us to the truth of the matter. It is absolutely true.

The Mediator of the New Covenant

In our previous studies on the Bible as a whole in what we call the aim and scope of the Bible, we have already pointed out the three-fold theme of the Scriptures—the Bringer of salvation, the way of salvation, and the saved.

I want to use these three—the Mediator of the covenant, the covenant in His blood, and the people of the covenant. I am not going to look up all these Scriptures related to it; we will just basically look at this three-fold theme which binds the old and the new covenants together. First of all, we will look at the Mediator of the covenant. It is very interesting that whether it is the old or the new, the Mediator of the covenant is the same. If you look at these Scriptures, Matthew 1:1–17 and Luke 3:23–38 you will find that they are all genealogies. You might question: what is all this huge number of verses with those weird sounding names like the son of so and so, and the son of so and so and the son of so and so? The whole point is this: the books of the New Covenant are being related systematically to the books of the Old Covenant. So when you come to the books of the New Covenant in Matthew 1:1, you are immediately taken right back to Abraham: "The book of the genealogy of Jesus Christ, the son of David, the son of Abraham." It goes straight back all that way.

Again, in Hebrews 8:6, and 1 Timothy 2:5 it speaks of Christ as the mediator of a new covenant. The Messiah is the focal point of the Old Covenant, and the Saviour is the focal point of the New

Covenant, and the Messiah Saviour or the Saviour Messiah is the focal point of the whole Bible. It is so simple. If you use another word for the Hebrew, "Messiah," the Greek, "Christ," then you have got it. The Christ is the focal point of the Old Covenant, the Saviour of the world is the focal point of the New Covenant, and the Saviour Christ is the focal point of the whole Bible. It does not matter where you turn; it is the heart of the whole thing. He binds the two covenants together. Do you honestly believe that it was the blood of lambs and bulls and goats that saved the people in the Old Covenant? Not at all! That high priest going into the presence of God once a year could not actually bring God near to the people or the people. It was because he represented Christ. That is the whole point.

Do you remember how the Lord Jesus in Luke 24:27, 44–45 spoke of Himself in all the Scriptures? "Then opened He their understanding of the Scriptures," that they might understand Him in all three great sections of the Old Covenant—the Law, the Prophets and the Psalms or the Writings. Remember how He spoke to the ones on the road to Emmaus? He told them of all things concerning Himself that were written in the Scriptures. It is all there. The whole Old Testament, all the books of the Old Covenant speak of Christ.

Have you ever thought how immeasurably poorer we would be if we did not have the books of the Old Covenant? if we did not have the messianic prophecies in the books of the Old Covenant? Supposing we never had that prophecy about the seed of the woman crushing the serpent's head and the serpent bruising or crushing the Saviour's heel. We would be much the poorer. Supposing we did not have Isaiah 53 or Psalm 22? Supposing we did not have those prophecies in Zechariah and Micah; we would be much the poorer for it. Isn't it a great encouragement to our faith that we have detailed predictions of the coming Christ in the books of the Old Covenant and we know they have been fulfilled? I say we would be immeasurably poorer; we would not be without our salvation, but we would be immeasurably poorer.

Again, supposing we did not have the passages of the coming glory of the kingdom of the Lord Jesus. For instance, take Isaiah; some of us live in Isaiah. Think of the coming glory of the coming kingdom. You would not find any of that in the New Testament. The Lord left it to the prophets of the Old Testament to tell us about the coming glories. We have touches of it in Romans 8 and I Thessalonians. We have some real touches in Revelation of the glory which is to come, but it is in the prophetical books of the Old Covenant that we really have an explanation, a definition of the coming glory and kingdom of our Lord Jesus. I say we would be so much poorer.

Think of Ezekiel, of Isaiah, of Micah, of Zephaniah—these wonderful prophecies of the coming glory of the Lord Jesus. Then think of I Chronicles from chapters 1–9. The whole first nine chapters of the first book of Chronicles is taken up with genealogies. They are so dry and so dusty, you might well ask yourself: What are they doing in Scripture? But the whole point is that on their own they mean nothing, but when you put them in with the books of the New Covenant they mean something, for they are the systematic vindication of the coming Christ. Now, this may not mean a lot to you, and it may not mean a lot to me, but it meant a tremendous lot to the Jews in the days of the early church. They were prejudiced against Christ—a crucified Messiah? That is a contradiction in terms. But the writings of the apostles gave so much place to these genealogies, which fully authenticated the line of Christ. They showed that He not only came from Abraham and beyond Abraham of course to Adam, but they showed that He was of the royal house of David, that He was born in Bethlehem. They were careful to authenticate the claims of the Lord Jesus to be the Christ. That is why you have genealogies in 1 Chronicles chapters 1–9 so you can compare them. While you may have some difficulties, and you will have some difficulties, nevertheless the general outline remains and they are something that fully authenticates the claims of the Lord Jesus.

We could say a good deal more about the Lord Jesus as Mediator of the covenant in the Old Testament, as we call it, and in the New. I will ask you just one more question: Do you think we would ever really understand, either as modern Jews or as modern Gentiles, what the priesthood of Christ means if we did not have the thirty-nine books of the Old Covenant? What would it mean to you? What would it mean to me? It would not mean a lot, I can tell you. What is a priest? What does he do? Muslim priest? Buddhist priest? Hindu priest? Roman Catholic priest? What kind of priest is Christ? We have the thirty-nine books of the Old Covenant and there we can discover the glories of His priesthood. There we can discover the absolute security that we have, as it were, rooted within the High Priesthood of the Lord Jesus Christ. What a wonderful thing it is to have someone who appears before God's face for us!

The Covenant in His Blood

Then again there is this second side—the covenant in His blood. In Revelation 5:6 it says, "... a lamb slain before the foundation of the world." And John 1:29: "Behold the Lamb of God who bears away the sin of the world." What do you think those hearers of John the Baptist thought when suddenly he took a turn, which meant something to them all in their very history? It would not have meant anything to Gentiles, but John the Baptist said to those Jewish people: "Behold, the Lamb of God who bears away the sins of the world." What would it have meant to us if we did not have the books of the Old Covenant? What do you think the Lord Jesus meant at the Passover when He said, "This cup is the new covenant in my blood"? It had behind it the ancient centuries-old tradition of the Passover. There it was on the table, the Lamb, and there was the bread; it's all there. Some authorities believe, in fact, that the Lamb was absent on that last great Passover of the Lord Jesus, with even greater symbolism and meaning. He Himself was the Lamb. "Take," He said, "this cup; drink ye all of it; this is the blood of the New Covenant." I think it is tremendous when you understand that— the covenant in His blood—the Lamb slain, precious blood shed. The death of an innocent victim underlies the whole of the Bible from Genesis to Revelation and it binds the two great divisions of the Bible into one.

I would like to ask a few questions very quickly. How could we understand so much of atonement if we did not have the books of the Old Testament, the Old Covenant? How would you and I understand the fullness of what Christ has done in His offering of Himself if we did not have the burnt offering? the peace offering? the sin offering? the trespass offering? Where are these in the New Testament? We have them in the Old Covenant, and there we understand something of the fullness of what Christ did for us on the cross.

What would we understand by this word covenant if we did not have the books of the Old Covenant? What would we understand by it? And what about the blood of Christ that is for cleansing, for covering, to making us nigh? Supposing we really did not have the books of the Old Covenant, and we did not know that everything in the temple was sprinkled with blood. We would not know how a leper could be cleansed in the temple if we did not know what was done with the blood on the Passover day, and so on. How much poorer we would be! I am saying all of this just that you might understand that the books of the Old Covenant are as essential as the books of the New. I am taking time over it, not because I think you do not know how essential they are, but simply because you ought to know the ground, the foundation for our beliefs that they are essential.

The People of the Covenant

Then there is the third strand, the people of the covenant. Hebrews 11:39–40: "And all these, though well attested by their faith, did not receive what was promised, since God had foreseen something better for us, that apart from us, they should not be made perfect."

That is tremendous really because it is continuity. Those saints under the Old Covenant are absolutely with us. It is wonderful, simply wonderful, and there is the continuity. They were not allowed to receive the promise fully because God wanted them to become perfect by our being included. That is wonderful!

Again in Acts 7:38, Stephen, in his great message to the Sanhedrin, speaks of the church in the wilderness. Unfortunately, our Authorized Version has translated the Hebrew word for church as "congregation" whereas the Greek translators used the word ecclesia, which we know as church. In the New Testament they translated this word as church so we have no continuity in the Authorized Version. We have in the Old Testament the congregation of the people of Israel, the children of Israel, and in the New Testament we have the church. But readers of the Greek Old Testament, and most of the early church were Greek-speaking and Greek readers, saw immediately the continuity for when they opened the pages of the Old Covenant in Greek they found ecclesia everywhere. Right back in the days of Moses they found the ecclesia in the wilderness and then all the way through they found it. Then when the Lord Jesus said, "I will build my ecclesia upon this rock," they understood. And when Paul began to talk about the ecclesia, they understood. It is all very wonderful when you begin to see it like that.

Hebrews 11:10 says, "Abraham sought the city which has the foundations."

Hebrews 12:22–23: "Ye are come unto Mount Zion to the new Jerusalem ..." Abraham sought it and we have come to it. It is wonderful.

In Revelation 21:12, 14, we are told that in one part of the wall we have the twelve names of the tribes of Israel and then we are told that in another place we have the twelve names of the apostles. What does it mean? It means the elect of the Jews and the elect of the Gentiles in one city. It is an amazing thing. No more Jew, no more Gentile but one new man.

Now it is this people of the covenant that is so marvellous. The early church saw that it was one company of the redeemed, whether under the Old Covenant or under the New Covenant.

In Galatians 3:7, it says that we are all sons of Abraham by faith. In chapter 6:16, Paul prays that this blessing might be upon the Israel of God.

The Origin of Every Major Biblical Idea

Thus we have this three-fold strand in Scripture. Without the Old Covenant we are in grave danger of misunderstanding many things in the New Covenant, or at least not having a balanced understanding of things in the New. Nearly every major Biblical idea or conception finds its origin in the Old Covenant. That is a very, very big statement to make, but it is absolutely true.

We also need the books of the Old Covenant in other ways. For example, take the book of Revelation. When I think, without being unkind, of some of the nonsense that has been written on the book of Revelation, some of the wild things that have been done on supposed revelations from the book of Revelation, one can only reemphasize this more strongly than ever. The book of Revelation can never be understood without an understanding of some of the books at least of the Old Covenant.

For instance, this idea of Babylon in the book of Revelation. In John's day Babylon ceased to exist, so what is he talking about? What does he mean by Babylon, which he called the great mother of harlots? He tells us about this great city where all the great merchants of the world come, all the merchandise, where all the commerce is centered, this great thing called Babylon. How can you understand it? There have been some wild, wild identifications of Babylon with various things. But if you go right back into the Old Covenant in Genesis you will find that Nimrod founded Babylon, and there was a tower called "Babel" that is connected with Babylon. As you go on through Scripture, step by step there is a development of something. You begin to understand that Babylon is the seat of world government, of world power. Then you discover that Babylon is not just a place in scriptural language; it has become a symbol of the whole world in all its genius, in all its nobility, in all its cruelty, in all its evil and unrighteousness.

Look at the book of Revelation, and suddenly you discover that this Babylon in the end is in final and terrible collision with another city, the city of Jerusalem. Jerusalem was destroyed and ceased to be the city of God. It is true that it is still sort of lingering on, but what has happened to Jerusalem? If you go back to the books in the Old Testament, you can trace the whole history of Zion. You go back to Abraham when he offered his only son Isaac on Mount Moriah, and you discover that it became in the end the place of the temple. You go on and go on, and gradually, you discover how the city of the Jebusites became Jerusalem, until it becomes not an earthly city anymore. It is Jerusalem which is above, the mother of us all. In many ways it is a wonderful example of what I am trying to say.

How can you understand the book of Revelation without Ezekiel? How can you understand the book of Revelation without Daniel? Take those visions in Daniel. There is a lion, a bear, a leopard, and an exceeding ferocious creature which we are not told what it is; it is so diverse and so terrible. Then come to the book of Revelation and we discover all four are rolled into one. Is that coincidence? How can you understand it? When I think of the things that in my short lifetime I have heard about some of these things, how one was Hitler, one was Stalin, and before that it was Mussolini and the fact that Mussolini was going to erect a great statute outside of Rome and all the rest of it. The whole point is you have to go back into the Old Testament to really discover something of the origin of these symbols and figures, and then you begin to understand their development in the hands of the Holy Spirit until you come to Revelation which is a kind of climax of it all.

Take the cherubim. It is an amazing fact that John did not call them cherubim; he called them living creatures. Someone said to me once they thought that John deliberately concluded the Scriptures, and that he sat down and wrote his book as the final chapter to the Bible. I think he did it rather badly in one or two ways, if he did do that. For one thing why did he not call them cherubim? In his vision he saw these living creatures or living ones as he calls them that have eyes all over and are continually moving. When you begin to look into them you suddenly get a shock. You turn back and discover to your amazement that in Ezekiel you have a much more detailed description of these living creatures, and there they are called "cherubim." That gives you an understanding, doesn't it? It saves you from a misinterpretation of Scripture.

We think of Zechariah and his visions, and Malachi and his. We talked about John the Baptist and the witness and the olive trees in Zechariah. How are we going to understand that chapter in Revelation because somewhere or other there is a strange link with Zechariah and Malachi? So if we are going to understand the book of Revelation, which is the consummation of the whole of the Bible in God's hand—it is in fact that, although I do not believe John meant it to be wholly that—we have to go back to the books of the Old Covenant and understand these things. We have to find out what they mean and then trace their course through until we come to the end.

Without the books of the Old Covenant, the symbols, the figures, and types used in the New have little meaning or are open to misinterpretation. Suffice it to say that here we have sixty-six books and they are sixty-six parts of one organic unity. It is as if you could say, with the body, "Cut off a hand." Yes, you can do without one hand or you can do without one leg. But if you want fullness of life, you need that leg; you need that hand, and so it is with these books of the Bible. They are all part of a fullness of a living organic unity. Every part is vital. Every part has a function to perform in the full revelation of God's heart and mind, and so we have this great major division into two. However, we must not think that the books of the Old Covenant are inferior to the books of the New. It is a subtle, insidious mistake to make. They are as inspired and as authoritative as the books of the New. They are necessary one to the other. I hope the Lord will have helped us a little in our understanding of the structure and growth of the Bible.

7.
The Arrangement of the Books of the Bible

We have spent time considering the name "Bible." First, we have seen that the Bible is a library of sixty-six books and that it has a major two-fold division, which we call testaments, the Old and the New Testament. More correctly they should be called covenants—thirty-nine books of the Old Covenant and the twenty-seven books of the New.

Now we come to the arrangement of the books. How did these sixty-six books come to their present position? There are three main arrangements of the books of the Bible. There is the Hebrew arrangement, there is what we call the Septuagint arrangement, which is the oldest translation of the Old Testament into Greek before Christ, and there is the final or Christian arrangement of the books of the whole Bible. These are the three main arrangements of the books of the Bible. The whole subject of the way in which the various books came to occupy their final positions is absolutely fascinating. Of course, we will only be able to touch on it. I am not a great enough authority to be able to go into all the ins and outs of the way these books came to their final position or indeed how they finally came to be included in the canon. However, we shall cover the main points.

Firstly, we shall look at the Hebrew arrangement of the Old Testament. It is the Hebrew arrangement that the Jews of our Lord's day were acquainted with, and have been acquainted with ever since. Then we shall deal with the Septuagint or Hellenist arrangement of the Old Covenant along with the final and Christian arrangement. I ought just to say that within these three main arrangements there was a very great variation in the position of individual books, and we shall look at that as we go along. Although the three main arrangements have general outlines, there was quite a variation of order within those general outlines.

The Hebrew Arrangement of the Old Covenant

First of all, we shall look at the Hebrew arrangement of the books of the Old Covenant, and you will see straight away that it is a three-fold arrangement. The Lord Jesus spoke of this arrangement, when after His resurrection He spoke of those things concerning Himself in the Law, the Prophets, and the Psalms. Sometimes the title of the Psalms was "The Psalms," but more technically it was called "The Writings." The Psalms were the first and major part of the last division of the Hebrew arrangement of the Bible. This was the Bible that the Lord Jesus used. It was the arrangement of the books that He was acquainted with when He discussed with the doctors of the Law in the temple as He was about to commence His Father's business, in His Father's house. It is three-fold. First is the Law, or what even today the Jews still refer to as the Torah.

That, of course, is the first five books of the Bible, sometimes called "The Five Books of Moses" or by their Greek names—Genesis, Exodus, Leviticus, Numbers, and Deuteronomy. Those five books, in that order, comprised the Law.

The Prophets were subdivided into two. There were only four books in what they called the former prophets—Joshua, Judges, the two books of Samuel, which were one book in the Jewish arrangement, and the two books of Kings which were one book. The second division of the prophets was the latter prophets, which were Isaiah, Jeremiah, Ezekiel, and then the twelve that we call the minor prophets. These were gathered by the Jews into one book. You have Isaiah, Jeremiah, Ezekiel—three books—and then the fourth, entitled "The Twelve."

The third division, the Writings, was subdivided into three. The first subdivision consisted of the Psalms followed by Proverbs, followed by Job. In other words, there you have, more or less, the poetic or wisdom literature of the Old Testament. The second subdivision was called "The Five Scrolls" or the Megillot, still used in Jewish circles today. The five scrolls are the Song of Solomon, Ruth, Lamentations, Ecclesiastes, and Esther. The last subdivision of this third major division of the Old Testament of the Hebrew arrangement was Daniel, Ezra, Nehemiah—one book, and Chronicles. (We will not call it the Jewish Bible because that would be unfair since the Hellenist arrangement of the Bible was also Jewish. Remember, Paul calls himself a Hebrew of Hebrews, whereas Stephen was a Hellenist.) We call this the Hebrew arrangement.

How did this three-fold Hebrew division of the books of the Old Covenant take place? We cannot, in fact, with any certainty state its origin. It is often suggested that these three divisions, the Law, the Prophets, and the Writings, represent the three-stages of growth in the Old Testament and its recognition as canonical. This is the oft-repeated statement—first the Law, then the Prophets, then the Writings.

It is interesting to note the fact that in this Hebrew arrangement, we have in the first five books, roughly, the nucleus of the Old Testament faith, the absolute hard core of the Old Testament faith. Then in the next division, the Prophets, both former and latter, we have an objective expansion and interpretation. That is, it defines how you go wrong objectively and how you get into the right objectively. For instance, you can point out from Saul how you go wrong and then from David how you can go right. You are objectively pointing it out. In Samson you show what God could have done in him and what he did with himself. Objectively, it is an expansion of God's Law. God says certain things in His law; it is the hard core of the Old Testament faith.

In this next section, the Prophets, you begin to find that the prophets who wrote the history as well as the prophets who prophesied, brought out God's Word in a living way. They both have this as their objective to point out and define what is right and what is wrong to illustrate in lives. It is a very, very interesting point. The former prophets are not what many of you would call prophets— Joshua, Judges, Samuel, and Kings. You would say they are history, but the old rabbis said they were not history and put them under the prophets. (They had a reason for it that we will come to.) It was really an expansion in an objective way of what was found in the first five books.

We could say the last division, the Writings, was a subjective expansion and interpretation of the first five books. Take Psalms;

it is all subjective. It is what is happening inside. Think of the Psalmist; he is pouring out his heart in a subjective way. What about Job? It is very subjective; it is all that is happening inside the man. Proverbs, in one way, is subjective, but it is objective as well. It is not wholly true of these three books in Jewish arrangement, but nevertheless it is a very interesting thought that lies behind it. Roughly, you have first the nucleus of the Old Testament faith, then the expansion and interpretation in an objective way of that faith, and thirdly, an expansion and interpretation of that faith subjectively.

The Law

Whatever we may feel about that we can say that the Law, the first five books, was called by the Jews, "The Five Fifths." Because they saw it as a whole, they called it colloquially "The Five Fifths." These five books were associated with one another in their main body from a very early date indeed and were the first to be recognised together as a body of books. There seems to be no variation down through the centuries in the order of these first five books right through to today. There has never been a variation of this order—Genesis, Exodus, Leviticus, Numbers, Deuteronomy. It is an amazing fact, and there has been very little controversy over it.

The Prophets

The second division, the Prophets, is interesting since it contains a large amount of history. As I have pointed out, the former prophets—Joshua, Judges, Samuel, and Kings were mostly history, and not what you and I would call prophecy. These books were not included here merely because prophets were responsible for their writing. In fact the prophets did write them, but that was not merely the reason why they were included here. They were included here because the rabbis said it was history interpreted, and that is prophecy. I hope you get hold of that because some people have got the weirdest ideas of prophecy. They think it is all prediction. It does include prediction, but it is not only prediction. Prophecy is the interpretation of things in a situation bringing it right home. That is why they were included here, not only because they were written by prophets, but because it was history interpreted.

This is true of Joshua to Kings. It is history interpreted, not just ordinary history. In the book of Kings we will find things such as, "this king did not destroy the high places." That is not just history; that is history interpreted. Because he did not do that, later on you will discover what happened. Joshua tells you all that the people of God possessed of the Promised Land and it also very quietly says, " ... and they did not possess this ... and they did not possess that." Just very quietly it says in one place that because there were chariots of iron there, they could not possess it. But when you come to Judges, it tells you all that they did not possess and how the very part they did not possess was used by the devil to take what they had possessed, so that they went back into slavery. Now, that is history interpreted. Then we have the whole story of Saul and David, and it is not just a story of one bad king or one good king, but it is history interpreted. That is why it was included by the rabbis under the term "The Prophets." (The rabbis were not as silly as some people think.)

The latter prophets contain prophecy as we generally understand it. The main point of interest here is the exclusion of Daniel.

I would imagine this should raise great difficulty with you all. Of all the books of the Bible, if I asked you to give me an example of a prophetic book, I would expect most of you to say Daniel. But the rabbis did not include Daniel in the prophets. It is a most remarkable thing. They did not feel he should be there, which is a real point of interest. Another point of interest is that the twelve Minor Prophets were all gathered together into one book, into one volume in the Jewish arrangement. We should also note that there was a certain amount of variation in the order of the books in the latter prophets. For instance, sometimes Isaiah does not come first but Jeremiah comes first. It varied.

The Writings

The third division is "The Writings." They are a little more difficult to understand because they seem to be almost miscellaneous. This division has the greatest variation in the order of its books. We can understand why the Psalms were included in this division because the Psalms were the hymnal of the Old Testament church. It was their hymnbook, and that is why they were included here. We can understand Proverbs because it is a collection of proverbs. We can understand Job being put here because it is a drama in many ways. We can understand all that; it is what we call wisdom literature. We can also understand the five scrolls or five little books being here—Song of Solomon, Ruth, Lamentations, Ecclesiastes, and Esther. They were gathered together because each one was read separately on five great occasions in the life of God's people annually. First, the Song of Solomon was always read at Passover. All Jews heard the scroll of the Song of Songs read at the Passover in all synagogues to this day. Ruth was always read at Pentecost. Lamentations, as one would expect, was read on the anniversary of the destruction of Jerusalem. Ecclesiastes was read, very interestingly, at the Feast of Tabernacles, which is a feast of fullness. It is very interesting that Ecclesiastes, which is "Vanity, vanity, all is vanity," should be read at that point to remind people. Esther was always read, as we would expect, at the Feast of Purim, which commemorates the deliverance of the Jews in the days of Esther. These books are still read today in every synagogue. If you go into the synagogue in Richmond at Passover, you hear the Song of Solomon. And if you go at Pentecost, you will hear Ruth, and so on.

We can understand how these two divisions came together in "The Writings," but it is not so easy to understand why Daniel is here. Why do you think Daniel was put there? Why do you think Ezra and Nehemiah were put there and Chronicles is the most remarkable one of all. It is absolutely unchronological. Chronicles comes first and then Ezra follows. The last verses of the last chapter of II Chronicles are the first verses in Ezra. Isn't it remarkable that the rabbis, or whoever it was, tore away Chronicles and put it last? Why? It was because Chronicles finished the Hebrew Old Testament. So if a saint under the Old Covenant was reading the Scriptures just before the days of our Lord, he would have started with Genesis and worked through, and when he came to the last scroll, he would have finished at Chronicles. It is most interesting.

We can say that these last books are all to do with the end times. Is that why they are put there? The last three are history and they are history interpreted, so they should be with the prophets. Some say they were not written by a prophet. There may have been a point to that; they were written by a priest. Daniel, by the way, was neither a prophet nor a priest. He was a statesman; he was Prime Minister actually. Some people say that is why those books are there, but surely there must be a spiritual meaning in the way these books came to occupy the last spot.

Of course, I think you all know Daniel is all to do with the times of the Gentiles right down to the end of world history. We can find ourselves truthfully, without being fanciful, in the book of Daniel. It deals with the times of the Gentiles; and we are in the times of the Gentiles now. Ezra and Nehemiah deal with recovery. Chronicles also deals with recovery, but it deals with the whole battle over the temple. You remember the two books of Samuel and Kings deal with the same things as Chronicles, but they deal with the throne and the king, and Chronicles deals with the temple and its services. The last book of this Hebrew arrangement of the Old Covenant deals with the heart of God's purpose, which is a house for the Lord, a temple in which He might dwell.

The Septuagint Arrangement and the Christian Arrangement

We will go on to the final arrangement—the Septuagint (or Hellenist) and the Christian arrangement of the books of the Old and the New Covenant. There is the Pentateuch—Genesis, Exodus, Leviticus, Numbers, Deuteronomy, which correspond to the Law.

The historical books are Joshua, Judges, Ruth, I and II Samuel, split into two, I and II Kings, split into two, I and II Chronicles, which was a new addition, Ezra and Nehemiah, a new addition, and Esther, a new addition.

The poetic books are Job, Psalms, Proverbs, Ecclesiastes, and Song of Solomon.

The prophetical books are Isaiah, Jeremiah, Ezekiel, Daniel, and the twelve Minor Prophets as separate books from Hosea to Malachi. That is the final arrangement for both the Hellenist or Septuagint and Christian Bible.

The Old Covenant

We will look first at the Old Covenant. The first thing I want you to note is that the final arrangement of the books of the Old Covenant came to us via the Septuagint and the Latin Vulgate. Why was there a Greek version of the Old Testament? It goes back to a terrible division that took place in God's people under the Old Covenant. The Hebrews, as they were called, were the ones who went back to Palestine in the Promised Land to build the temple. They lived there and brought up their children, and their descendants were there. The others all remained in what was called "the dispersion." These folk of the dispersion became much more free, much more sort of broad-minded, much more "go ahead" than their contemporaries in the Promised Land. The Hebrews were looked upon as rather prejudiced, rather narrow, rather conservative and old-fashioned. So we get these two streams amongst God's people, the Hebrews and the Hellenists.

After a while the Hellenists no longer spoke Hebrew or Aramaic, and therefore they clamoured for a version of God's Word in the tongue that they were speaking, which was Greek. So it came about that the Old Testament was translated into Greek, much to the horror of the Hebrews who looked upon Hebrew as the language of

God. They felt it was the most terrible, despoiled sacrilege to take the sacred Hebrew of the Scriptures and translate it into a vulgar tongue like Greek. But in fact this vulgar tongue was to influence the final arrangement of the books very, very greatly indeed. The Septuagint, as we call it, or the Hellenist arrangement, was a roughly chronological one, evidently rearranged into a chronological order. Whether it was based, as some scholars believed, on older Hebrew arrangements we cannot dogmatically say. There are scholars who believe that the current Hebrew arrangement was only one among others and that the Hellenist arrangement, in fact, embodies an even older tradition and may even precede that arrangement. The Septuagint is the arrangement that our Lord Jesus knew. He refers to it at least once, if not more than that, in what He said.

In this rearrangement of the Hebrew Bible there were many variations, but it finally resolved itself into the arrangement we have today. We must note one or two things. Ruth has been taken away from "The Five Scrolls" and placed where she belongs at the end of Judges. In fact, it is a great probability that she was written by the same person who wrote Judges. Then again, I want also to note that Chronicles, Ezra, and Nehemiah are moved to where they should be in roughly, approximately chronological order—I and II Chronicles, Ezra, Nehemiah, and Esther. In fact, to be absolutely right, Esther should come in the middle of Ezra, but we cannot do that. They put I and II Chronicles, Ezra, Nehemiah, and Esther at the end. That seems to be good. Then they took Lamentations and put it back with Jeremiah where it belonged. Not all scholars would agree with that, but certainly in thought it belongs there. Then, of course, our dear friend Daniel is taken away from the Writings and put where he belongs, with the Prophets.

It is a very interesting rearrangement of the Hebrew Scriptures that the Greek-speaking rabbis indulged in. I am sure that it was not just an indulgement; it was obviously under the hand of the Holy Spirit for this is the arrangement that finally came to us. It is interesting because as you know we have Isaiah who spanned the whole range of prophecy. Then we have Jeremiah, Ezekiel, and Daniel, the prophets of recovery, the three great ministers of recovery. Of course we expect Malachi to be where he is at the end of the Old Covenant. All those things we understand.

The New Covenant

We come to the New Covenant. The Gospels are Matthew, Mark, Luke, and John. The Historical book, Acts. The Didactical books are Romans, I and II Corinthians, Galatians, Ephesians, Philippians, Colossians, I and II Thessalonians, I and II Timothy, Titus, Philemon, Hebrews, James, I and II Peter, I, II, III John, and Jude. (Didactical is a dreadful word. I tried to get away from it, but wherever you read you will find this dreadful word. It just means teaching.) Then prophetic book, Revelation. That is the arrangement that has come to us of the books of the New Covenant.

The twenty-seven books of the New Covenant consist of five narrative books and twenty-one letters. Some of the letters are small personal letters, such as II and III John and Philemon; some of them are mighty treatises, such as Hebrews, Romans, Galatians, and Ephesians. They are letters but they are tremendous. That brings it to twenty-six books and we have one final book of visions, Revelation. It is quite unique in the New Covenant because it consists entirely of visions.

The Gospels

How did this arrangement come about? It is a very interesting study. The individual Gospels were originally circulating on their own in various localities. Mark, Peter's young companion, heard Peter preach again and again and again. In the end he sat down and wrote it. In all probability Peter corrected him as he wrote. It is the Gospel he had heard Peter preach all over the place, and we believe it was written in Rome.

Matthew was written in Palestine, and it circulated in Palestine, Judea, and Syria. It was based largely on a large collection of the Lord's sayings. It was very probably written by Matthew himself, if not completely, certainly the largest part of it.

Doctor Luke, Paul's companion, had heard Paul preach the Gospel so often he could have preached it himself no doubt if he had had the gift. He sat down with another clear-cut objective. He was not bothered about the Hebrews and he was not bothered about the Hellenists. He was a Gentile, not a Jew. Luke was a thorough-going Gentile, and he was bothered about the Greek-speaking Gentiles. So he sat down and wrote a two-volume history—Luke and Acts. Originally, they were bound together as one volume—part one and part two of one book. The doctor sat down and wrote his account of the Lord's life and death—the Gospel according to Luke and what we now call Acts. This circulated amongst Gentiles and it was very favoured by the Gentiles and all Greek-speaking people, Jews as well. We cannot be dogmatic, but it is probable that much of what Paul preached is in Luke's Gospel.

At the end of the first century, John wrote his Gospel after all the others had been written. I want to make this point very clear because John wrote it when he knew that those other Gospels were already circulating and many others as well, some spurious. He knew they were circulating. He sat down and wrote another Gospel, but this one was not covering the same ground as the others; it was supplementing them. That is very important. It was an interpretation. His whole objective was different from the other three Gospels, and that is very important to understand. It probably circulated in the churches in Asia Minor because John was in Ephesus, and that is where it would have gone.

By the beginning of the second century the four Gospels, one circulating in Syria and Judea, one in Rome, one in Asia Minor, and one amongst the Greek-speaking Gentiles, were brought together and bound together. They were called the Gospel according to Matthew, the Gospel according to Mark, the Gospel according to Luke, the Gospel according to John. In other words, they were brought together under one cover and when that happened, Acts was torn away from Luke and separated. In the arrangement of the books, it is a most amazing way in which these four different Gospels were written. Three of them were written, not in any way to complement each other, but were written in different parts and brought together, and then John's Gospel supplementing them and added to them. And what do you get? You get the most amazing four-fold picture of Christ. That is obvious and immediately reveals that the Holy Spirit is in this arrangement, for it was not humanly arranged.

It was not as if Peter sort of wrote a note to Matthew and said, "Look here, Matthew, you write down the life of the Lord, and I am going to get Mark to write it down, too. I am much busier than you are, Matthew; Mark will write one and you write one, and we will bring them both together." Not at all! But here is an even more amazing thing. Although the order within these four Gospels varied for a while, in the end it came to be the one we have now—Matthew, Mark, Luke, and John. The first two are King and Servant; the second two are Man and God. It is the most amazing thing, and when you look back to the cherubim, you have it—the head of the lion, the head of the ox, the head of a man, and the head of an eagle. It just cannot be a human arrangement. It is a most remarkable arrangement!

So again we have to admit that we are in the presence of a tremendous mystery. Where would we be if we only had Matthew? Where would we be if we only had John? We have this amazing four-fold picture of Christ. Matthew did not realise he was presenting Him as King wholly, and yet there is his emphasis. Mark did not wholly realise it was as Servant he was presenting the Lord. Luke, being a doctor, naturally it was the human side that appeared. Isn't it amazing? Of course, Paul's gospel is very much to do with the church, and the Lord is the Head of a new man. So it was man that was emphasised in Paul's gospel. We know that John emphasised the divinity of the Lord Jesus all the time. I can only bring this to you, and it is very, very wonderful!

When these four Gospels were brought together, Acts was separated from Luke and circulated on its own. Or sometimes it circulated with what we call "the catholic," not the Roman Catholic, but the catholic or general epistles which are James, Jude, I and II Peter. Sometimes Acts would circulate with them.

Paul's Letters

Paul's letters, which were amongst the first of the New Testament writings, were at the very beginning kept by the churches or individuals to whom they were addressed and circulated within the area. You remember when he wrote to Ephesus, he said let the folk at Laodicea see this letter and see that they show you the letter I sent to them. So they circulated in their own local areas, but they were kept by the churches or companies or individuals to whom they were addressed. By the end of the first century, all thirteen had been collected together under one cover and entitled "The Apostle." I do not know whether that was a dig at some of the others, but it came under the title "The Apostle." Everyone knew when they spoke about "The Apostle," that it was the writings of Paul.

Gradually, these collections came together—the four Gospels and the thirteen letters in "The Apostle." When they came together, what was more fitting than to put Acts between them because Acts linked up the Gospels with Paul. It linked up Peter, the supreme figure amongst the apostles in the Gospels with Paul, the supreme figure in the New Testament church. So Acts came in between and became the link between the two collections. As these collections came together, the arrangement we have now grew.

The Other Books

Revelation and Hebrews were the two major works over which there was much discussion and controversy, along with one or two of the small letters, II and III John, II Peter, Jude and one or two others. But the two major works were Revelation and Hebrews, and it was not until the fourth century after Christ that they were finally given universal recognition.

As this collection grew, there was much variation in the order in which individual books or letters were placed. Nowhere is this clearer than in the book of Revelation, which occupied various positions in the New Testament other than the concluding one. It is interesting that John the apostle never wrote Revelation to be the conclusion of the New Testament as some people think. He never wrote it as such. In fact, there was no New Testament at that point to conclude. So he could not have written it as the conclusion. Did he write it as a conclusion of the Old Testament? I do not think he would have done that. He saw these visions and he was commanded to put them into writing, and he obeyed. I am sure that as he did so he began to realise, "You know, this is, as it were, a conclusion of Ezekiel. This somehow seems to me to be the drawing together of Daniel and this seems to me to be the drawing together of threads in Zechariah, and Malachi, and Joel, and so on." He no doubt thought that, but he did not realise that he was writing what was destined to become the conclusion of the whole Bible. It was, in fact, under God's hand that after tremendous dispute, controversy, and variation of order the book of Revelation finally was placed at the end of the Bible, and rightly so. When you take the first three chapters of Genesis and the last three chapters of Revelation, there is a complete correspondence just as if nothing existed between. You would say whoever wrote the book of Revelation must have been doing it deliberately, and yet what you see here is evidence of the Holy Spirit in this work. This is just a little about the arrangement of the books. They are not there by chance; they are there by God's will, by God's placing.

The Canon of Scripture

Finally, we will consider a word or two about what we call the canon of Scripture. We have now covered something of the growth and structure of the Bible and the arrangement of the books, but we have got to ask ourselves a question. How was it decided which books should be included in these sixty-six books, and which should be excluded? Who made so solemn a decision, and when? Can we answer these questions? It is over these questions that we find and use the word "canon." All the books which are included are called canonical books and all those excluded are called apocryphal books.

The word canon came to us through Latin and Greek from a Semitic word which originally meant reed. In fact, you have it in Ezekiel where we are told that "a man took a measuring reed." That is the word. It is where we get our word canon through Latin and Greek. We get our English word "cane" from this Hebrew word canon. We get the word "canal" from it and its variation "channel." The idea is something straight; it is a reed. Because it was straight, the ancient world used this reed for measuring, as a measuring rod or a carpenter's rule. From there it came to be applied not only to that which measures, but to that which is measured. There is a whole growth of meaning in the word, and thus it came to have in the end two distinct meanings, which have great significance for us biblically.

The Meaning of Canon

The first meaning is index or list or catalogue. When we speak of the canon of Scripture, we speak of the catalogue of Scriptures, the list of Scriptures. You will see that in your Bible there is the canon of the Old Testament and the canon of the New. That is a list of all the books that are in the Bible, the sixty-six books. Canon also came to mean not only an index, a certain group or a number comprising something, but also had this other meaning of a rule or a standard or a law. It means the value and authority contained within those things, not only the actual list of things, but the actual intrinsic value, the intrinsic authority, of all that was in them. By the fourth century it had come to be applied to the Bible, which had arrived at its conclusive arrangement. The term covered not only the list of books recognised as inspired and authoritative which comprise our Bible, all sixty-six books, but also the authority of those books against all others as supremely authoritative in life, faith, and conduct. That is very important.

We must be clear that the books of the Bible have not become authoritative because they are canonical. They are canonical because they are divinely authoritative; that is very important. The Book itself has got divine authority within it, therefore it is canonical; it belongs to the Bible. If it has not got that divine authority and inspiration, then it is apocryphal, that is, not within the Bible.

We should also point out another thing. No church councils or other groups ever canonized Scripture. They may have canonized people, but they have never canonized Scripture ever. Never! They merely recognised what was already acknowledged over many years and in wide circles. This is very important to our understanding of what was included in the Bible and what was excluded.

The Canon of the Old Covenant

First, let's take the canon of the Old Covenant. The process was a long and gradual one. It would seem quite reasonable to state that it followed approximately the three divisions of the Hebrew arrangement. We have no dogmatic, definite authority to say that, but it would seem quite reasonable that it did, perfectly reasonable. Certainly, by our Lord's time the Old Covenant was complete. If you look at Luke 24:44 you will discover the Lord speaks of the Law, of the Prophets, and the Psalms. In other words, it was complete. By the way, the word "Psalms" there was used to cover the whole division, not just the book of Psalms.

There is another very interesting sidelight which reveals that it was complete. Do you remember in Luke 11:51 and Matthew 23:35, the Lord Jesus spoke of all the righteous blood shed from Abel to Zechariah. Why did he use Zechariah? In II Chronicles 24:21 you will discover the last martyr recorded in the Hebrew arrangement of the Bible was Zechariah and the first was of course Abel in Genesis 4:8.

So the Lord Jesus was simply saying He was taking the arrangement of the Hebrew Bible—the first martyr recorded was Abel, the last one was Zechariah. "I say to you that all of that blood would not be overlooked." He knew that it was not chronological; there were others who actually died chronologically after Zechariah. So this is a very interesting sidelight to the fact that they must have been complete by the time of our Lord.

It seems quite clear that our Lord, the apostles, and the New Testament church viewed the Old Testament in its Hebrew arrangement as divinely authoritative and inspired. Indeed, we must add that from the very beginning it would seem that the books that now comprise our Old Testament were recognised as authoritative and inspired. The very fact of debate over some of them reveals this. You know, the Jews love to debate. I think sometimes Gentile scholars tend to forget this. Jews love to haggle and always have done. There is nothing that a Jew likes more than a good thoroughgoing debate. The old rabbis were no exception. They were masters of debate, and they loved to have this open-air type of debate over anything; anything they could debate or dispute about. And that is how we got the Talmud from these disputations. Going back to this point, the very fact that the rabbis debated and disputed some of these books as to whether they were canonical or not reveals that they were very widely held as divinely and authoritatively inspired. Otherwise, they would not have bothered. It was just that they discussed whether it should be included or should not be included. It is included, but should it be? It was academic points that they were getting at.

The Three Main Divisions

Let's consider these three main divisions. First the Law; how did this come to be recognised? From the very beginning the Pentateuch was recognised as the Word of God. There may have been additions to it. Of course, Moses did not write the account of his own death; that is quite obvious. So there must have been additions to the first five books of the Pentateuch. However, it was the earliest part of God's Word to be officially recognised and probably at a very early date indeed, and with little, if any, controversy at all. Those first five books were recognised as the Law of God from the beginning, and anyone who contradicted it was in for a very, very bad time indeed, as far as God's people were concerned.

The second division, the Prophets, were in the main part recognised, it would seem anyway, by Ezra's time, which was the mid-fifth century BC. By the second century BC they were fully recognised, although over Ezekiel there was much debate. Why was there much debate and dispute over Ezekiel? It was due to his very involved divisions and the fact that the rabbis could not reconcile the account of the temple and its services in Ezekiel 40–48 with the Pentateuch. That reveals a very real critical acumen on the part of the rabbis. They were not as silly as some tend to think they were. That is why Ezekiel was discussed for a long, long time.

The third division, the Writings, is the one we have the greatest difficulty over. It seems certain that by our Lord's time it was officially recognised and in all probability much earlier. Yet as late as 70 AD when Jerusalem was being destroyed, there was heated debate amongst a certain school of rabbis over Esther because it was so thoroughly pagan. They wondered whether she should really be in the canon of Scripture at all. There was debate over Ecclesiastes because it was so unorthodox, especially the Pharisees did not like it at all; it seemed terribly worldly. There was a question about the Song of Songs because the New Testament rabbis were not exactly fond of Solomon. They felt he was rather immoral, and they really did wonder whether his Song about one of his loves should have ever got into Scripture. Again, with Proverbs it was partly to do with Solomon; they did not quite feel that he could have been so wise with that kind of life lying behind it. So there was great discussion even as late a date as that. But it is interesting to note that the conclusion of those debates in 70 AD established once and for all the divinely authoritative nature of those four books. There was an absolute recognition of those books as canonical.

The Apocryphal Literature

Now, just a few words about the apocryphal writers. There was a positive deluge of literature in the final years between Malachi and the Lord Jesus, and believe me, this is just a tiny fraction of apocryphal Old Testament literature: The Books of the Maccabees, The Wisdom of ben Sira, The Apocalypse of Ezra, The Wisdom of Solomon, The Book of Jubilee, The Apocalypse of Abraham, The Ascension of Isaiah (if you ever heard that he ascended), The Testament of the Twelve Patriarchs, The Apocalypse of Baruch, The Assumption of Moses, The Letter of Aristeas, and so on. All that is what we call apocryphal literature, and it was not included in the canon of the Old Testament.

The apocryphal writings, especially Tobias, Judah, the Wisdom of Solomon, Ecclesiasticus, the Prophecy of Baruch, I and II Maccabees are often included in Catholic versions and old Lutheran and Anglican versions of the Bible. Although these apocryphal writings were viewed in many cases as valuable and instructive, they were never accorded the same recognition by the rabbis as the canonical books of the Old Covenant. It was the uniform tradition of the Jews that Malachi ended prophetical and scriptural inspiration.

The Septuagint included a number of these apocryphal writings. The Greek-speaking rabbis, the Hellenist rabbis included them, but although they included them, Greek-speaking Jews never at any point looked upon them as canonical. They looked upon them as instructive and valuable but not as canonical in the same way that Luther said to include them at the end of the Old Testament." However, he wrote a little note to say these books are good for instruction; they are valuable, but they are not inspired and authoritative in the same way as the rest.

When Greek-speaking Gentile Christians began to read the Septuagint version, they tended to accept the whole as Scripture making no distinction, and thus these books passed into the Latin Vulgate. They passed from the Greek version into the Latin Vulgate and thus into our Bible. Generally, the greatest scholar amongst the church fathers was the one who clearly defined the difference. In fact, it is to him we owe the term apocryphal books. Nevertheless, the Roman Catholic Church, in 1500 and something I believe, finally accepted these books as canonical, which the reformers and the Protestants refused to do.

We must say that while there has been universal recognition and unanimity in the end over the thirty-nine books which comprised the Old Covenant from an early date, there has never been anything anywhere near unanimity on the apocryphal books of the Old

Testament. That is why we believe they did not have the testimony of the Holy Spirit as canonical.

The Canon of the New Testament

What can we say about the canon of the New Testament? The process of the New Testament canon was again like the Old Testament canon, a gradual one, but it did not take as long. Nearly the whole New Testament as we now have it was written by the end of the first century after Christ. The Lord Himself gave the promise that the Holy Spirit would lead the apostles into all truth. In John 14:26 Jesus says, "The Counselor, the Holy Spirit, whom the Father will send in my name, he will teach you all things, and bring to your remembrance all that I have said to you" (RSV). Isn't that wonderful? "… he shall teach you all things, and bring to your remembrance all that I said to you."

John 16:12, 13: "I have many things to say to you, but you cannot bear them now. When the Spirit of truth comes, he shall guide you into all the truth: for he shall not speak from himself; but what things soever he shall hear, these shall he speak: and he shall declare unto you the things that are to come" (RSV).

Will you note two verses of the Lord's own words? Past: "He will bring to remembrance all things that I said to you." Present: "He will lead you into all the truth" Future: "He will show you things to come." That comprises the whole New Testament. The New Testament is the written deposit of that truth that the Holy Spirit brought. Past—He will bring to remembrance all things that Jesus said—Matthew, Mark, Luke, John. Present—Acts and all the letters. "You cannot bear them now," He said. But through the Holy Spirit in the apostles and others, He taught them. So He led us into all truth. As Paul put it: "The truth as it is in Jesus" (see Ephesians 4:21). So we have all these books and letters from Acts right the way through to Jude, and it is all to do with the truth as it is in Jesus. Future—the Holy Spirit will show you things to come—the book of Revelation. It is a most amazing thing! The Lord Jesus covered the whole canon of the New Testament in this way.

In II Peter 3:15, 16 we read a most remarkable statement that Peter wrote: "And count the forbearance of our Lord as salvation. So also our beloved brother Paul wrote to you according to the wisdom given him, speaking of this as he does in all his letters. There are some things in them hard to understand, which the ignorant and unstable twist to their own destruction, as they do the other scriptures" (RSV). "… as they do the other scriptures." That is the most amazing thing. That word "scripture" is the word used of the Old Testament. Peter is speaking of Paul's writings as Scripture. As early as Peter, the writings of the apostle Paul were looked upon as Scripture. That is absolutely amazing!

By 140 AD, the Gospels, the Acts, and the Apostle (the writings of Paul), were looked upon as divinely inspired and authoritative and placed alongside the Old Testament canon. This meant eighteen books out of twenty-seven were thus considered canonical by the first half of the second century. There was only one exception and that was the Gospel according to John over which there was a great dispute toward the end of the second century. However, after that the Gospel of John was universally accepted, and it was about this time that for the first time the word New Testament came into use. It was used, not of all the books, but most of them, and they were called the books of the New Covenant or Testament. As early a date as that, they were looked upon as the Old Covenant with the books of the New Covenant already forming. One of the early church fathers used that term.

By 230 AD, only Hebrews, II Peter, II and III John, James and Jude were not recognised. They were the only ones, along with some apocryphal literature that some people felt should be included—The Shepherd of Hermas, The Didache, The Gospel of the Hebrews, The Epistle of Barnabas, and a few other things that some people thought should be included in the New Testament books. Revelation was more or less generally accepted by then.

By the fourth century, the twenty-seven books of the New Testament as we now have it were universally recognised. In the third Synod of the church at Carthage in 397 AD, it was said that besides these canonical Scriptures, nothing was to be read in the church under the title of divine Scripture. It is clear that apostolic authorship counted a tremendous amount with the early church, and it counted much in their recognition of these books as authoritatively inspired. This is the reason why there once was such a flood of apocryphal literature in the New Testament, which used names of the apostles. If you look through them you will be absolutely staggered by some of these things. There are gospels of this and gospels of that, epistles by so and so, and letters. It is absolutely amazing because everyone was trying to get things included, many of them heretical, a lot certainly erroneous. They were trying to get it into the church by using an apostle's name or one of the great church leaders' names. I think all scholarship agrees that this literature is nowhere near the New Testament standard, and it is very, very interesting how gradually what was inspired was brought in even though there was much debate and dispute. What was not inspired—though at one time there was the feeling that it should be kept in—was gradually pushed out until finally we have the books of the New Covenant, the canon of the New Covenant.

The Summary

What can we say to summarise all of what has been said? We can say that the canon of Scripture grew over many years and was searchingly selective. It was not by modern methods of criticism, but certainly, comparatively speaking, the rabbis did not just accept books "just like that." They debated them, they studied them, and they compared them. It was a searchingly selective test that was applied to these books. It is most interesting that no religious body or council, be it of the Jews or of the Christians, ever made Scripture or canonized books. They simply, officially recognised what was universally recognised already. To this we must add the inward testimony of the Holy Spirit to the divine authority and inspiration of these books in both the church and the individual from the beginning down through the years since and now.

Lastly, I might say that indeed the supreme wonder must be the oversight of the Holy Spirit in the whole process of the Bible's formation from its beginning to its end. It is a most fascinating subject, and we have only been able to touch upon it; there are many, many other lines we could profitably pursue. The one thing is that even with all the difficulties, in the most amazing way, the Lord uses centuries over centuries in different ways to finally, as it were, produce these sixty-six books of the Bible. I sometimes wonder whether, with the Psalmist who wrote Psalm 119, whether we share with him the same reverence and the same love for God's Word. It is an amazing volume indeed!

Study Guides

The Bible–Revelation, Inspiration, and Authority

A. Revelation

i. What do we mean by the word "revelation"? The Oxford Dictionary gives its meaning as "the disclosing of knowledge to man by divine or supernatural agency", whilst both the Hebrew and Greek words translated "to reveal," mean "to uncover, or unveil."

ii. The Bible is therefore the revelation of God Himself given by inspiration through men to man. It is the unveiling of God's character, purpose and salvation, both authoritative and unique. What the human mind and intellect could never attain to naturally; what was beyond man's ability to discover or understand, God has revealed.

iii. This unveiling of Himself is a progressive revelation. It begins with Genesis and is gradually unfolded, more and more fully, until the book of Revelation. Note carefully Hebrews 1:1–2. Mark "portions" and "manners" ASV, "fragmentary and varied" NEB, "Many and various ways" RSV.

It is the Revelation of God Himself given through:

a) Direct word – e.g. Exodus 25:1ff

b) Prophecy – e.g. Isaiah 53

c) History – (including miraculous events) national and personal. E.g. Exodus 13–14 Psalms and Job.

d) Types and Figures – e.g. Noah; pool of Marah; dove; serpent

e) Theophany – e.g. Exodus 19:16 ff; Gen 32:33 ff

f) The Lord Jesus Himself – He is the supreme and full revelation of God. See John 1:14, 16–18

g) The Body of Christ, the Church – The Revelation was completed with the New Testament written by the Holy Spirit through the Early Church, principally the apostles and prophets e.g. Ephesians 2:20, II Peter 3:15, 20 NB. v20, "the other Scriptures."

IV. This revelation is a unity. We need all the parts to fully understand the whole, and the whole to fully understand the parts. No one piece of Scripture can be isolated and "privately" interpreted. II Peter 1:20 (See particularly J.N. Darby's version of this and his foreword.) It must be compared and understood in the whole. It is dangerous to build a doctrine on an isolated verse, story or parable. In the revelation not every part is as important, profound or final, but all is necessary to the full revelation.

To neglect or ignore any part is harmful.

V. If then the Bible is an unveiling of God, beyond our natural ability to attain to or properly understand, it follows that we cannot approach it in an ordinary way, as we would Shakespeare, or Goethe or Tolstoy, etc. Revelation is a principle! It is not enough to have the Bible as the revelation of God! We must have the eyes of our hearts enlightened. Ephesians 1:17–18; Matt 16:17; II Corinthian 2:6–16. Self-sufficient knowledge is a great danger and stumbling block, stemming as it does from the fall. Upon that type of mentality and approach rests a divine veto. We need the gracious ministry of the Holy Spirit in our approach to the Word of God.

B. Inspiration

What do we mean by "Inspiration"? The Oxford Dictionary gives its meaning as "to breathe in," inhale; infuse thought or feeling into." This is not the Scriptural idea at all. The word used in II Timothy 3:16, means literally "God breathed" and means "breathed out" more than "breathed in. It is in fact important that we should understand the difference. The Bible is not the result of God infusing thoughts and feelings into certain men, playing on their artistic and "spiritual" abilities. The Bible resulted from God the Holy Spirit within them breathing out His mind and heart. See II Timothy 3:16; I Peter 1:10–11 "in them"; II Peter 1:19–21 "moved – borne along"; Hebrews 1:1 "God ... in the prophets ..." When we therefore speak of the divine inspiration of the Bible, we do not mean that it is inspiring or inspirable, nor that God is breathing through the Scripture nor that the Scriptures breathe out God, but that God has breathed out the Scripture. The Bible has been produced by God, by the Holy Spirit moving in certain men. It is therefore clear that the Bible is in a different class altogether to the inspired work of the human genius.

We must also note that this "inspiration" covers every part and phase in the "construction" of God's Word – human temperament and background; prevailing conditions and knowledge; transmission from the oral to the written. Note II Timothy 3:16, the word "Scriptures" is the technical word for "Writings."

iii. The Scriptural idea of inspiration does not, however, mean a mechanical dictation, or the putting aside of human personality and will. In this it differs from the Gentile view than the view which is prevalent and still lingering today, that inspiration means, "possession with human will suspended." It is interesting to note, in this connection, I Corinthians 14:32. Ecstasy there may be, and a complete lack of self-consciousness, but not the loss of self-control.

iv. This revelation of God, in a way which is impressive, has been given by the Holy Spirit in and through different men at different times in the style, method and vocabulary of their day. It is however this mysterious connection between the divine and human aspects of the Scripture which is both baffling and instructive. Note carefully II Peter 1:21 RSV. Here we are at the heart of the mystery, "No prophecy ever came by impulse of man but men moved by the Holy Spirit ..." Note also NEB version of this, "men they were, but impelled by the Holy Spirit ..." The word translated "moved" means "borne along, impelled." Compare Acts 27:15, 17 "were driven"; also Acts 2:2, "rushing"–all the same word.

V. This divine compulsion was neither physical, nor psychological. It certainly did not involve setting aside of the personality, character, or will of the human vessel. Indeed, it would seem that this divine direction and compulsion used the originality of the human author or speaker to the full, breathing through their particular personality and character quite naturally, and allowing them both spontaneity and freedom. Yet the outcome was "God-inspired Scripture." Note again carefully Mark 12:36–David's words and yet they are given "In the Holy Spirit." Compare Heb 1:13–the same Psalm quoted but no mention of David, only divine authorship. The book of Acts (see 1:16)–divine authorship again. Acts 2:25, 34–only human authorship. There are so many phrases–"Moses said; Moses wrote; Isaiah said; Isaiah cried; Isaiah did prophecy; Scripture said; God said" etc. It is not that there are various depths and differing measures of divine inspiration. Studied carefully, it will be seen that all is equated within "God said"

Again it is instructive to note that when God wishes to give us a full orbed view of His Son, He takes four different men who say the same thing in different ways! Matthew, Mark, Luke and John. If inspiration were a mechanical dictation, one writer could have sufficed and would have saved us a number of difficulties. It is virtually the same with the letters. God takes a Paul to speak to us about faith, and a James to speak to us about works! He takes a John to speak to us about eternal security and a writer of the Hebrews about losing our inheritance! Yet all is equally God inspired!

Then again note the difference in style between Genesis, Daniel and Song of Songs; or Isaiah and Ezekiel; or John, Paul and James. Or the differences in method between the acrostic Psalms e.g. 34, 37, 119; composite (Mosaic) Psalms e.g. 144; between Psalms 22, 42, and Job, Proverbs and Zechariah; Song of Songs (allegory) and Exodus; Romans, Philemon, James; Revelation and Acts.

Or the differences in vocabulary between Genesis 1 and Ephesians 1; Ezekiel and Isaiah; John's letters and Paul's letters.

Or the difference in personality between Jacob, Moses, David, Isaiah, Jeremiah, Daniel, Luke, Paul, James, Peter. The personality of the writer is not obliterated by divine inspiration at all! (Note for interest Rev 1:9, II Corinthians 10:1) At times it would seem that the very failings of the individual, or should we say their temperamental lacks, are used by God, e.g. Jeremiah, Paul and James. It seems therefore quite clear that inspiration does not mean sameness of style, or method, or vocabulary, or of temperament.

VIII. All these men had one thing in common. They were chosen, apprehended, prepared and anointed by the same Lord as vessels through which he would produce the Scriptures. Were they always conscious and aware of this "inspiration"? See I Peter 1:10–11, RSV; John 8:56; Galatians 3:8; Hebrews 11:13–16, etc.; Acts 2:30, 31 NEB. But what about Job; Jonah; Psalm 22; Psalm 51– both David's; Paul in II Corinthians 7:8; Philemon?

IX. In all that we have said the supreme thing about the Bible is its divine authorship. We are not handling something which merely contains God's Word, or something which merely breathes God. We are handling the Word of the Lord given us by divine inspiration. An argument with Scripture invariably involves us, in the end, in an argument with God.

C. Authority

i. What do we mean by "Authority"? The Oxford Dictionary gives its meaning as "the power, right to enforce obedience." We therefore mean that the Word of God has the incontestable power and right to claim our absolute obedience, to settle all questions and matters in dispute, and to mould and fashion us in every part of our life.

The authority of the Bible lies wholly in the fact that it claims divine authorship. It claims to be "The Word of the Lord," a God given revelation, with the inherent power to accomplish His will. It is not merely literary, not merely ethical, nor merely outlining the truth. It is the powerful and creative Word of God Himself, living and active. Psalm 119:50; Isaiah 55:11; John 15:3; Acts 19:20; II Corinthians 4:6; Ephesians 5:26; 6:17; Hebrews 1:3; 4:12; 11:3; James 1:18; I Peter1:21–25; II Peter 3:5, 7.

There are three ways in which we see this claim to authority:

a) The Old Testament is full of phrases such as "God spoke;" "God said"; "The Word of the Lord came;" "Thus said the Lord," etc. It has been estimated that there are 3,800 such references. To these we must add all the acts of God with which its pages are filled remembering that those acts are all with meaning. We must also add the appearances of God. The sum of it all adds up to a divinely initiated, inspired and authenticated revelation.

b) Christ Himself witnessed to this authority. John 10:35 (cannot be broken); Luke 22:37 (must be fulfilled); Matt 5:17–19; Matt 22:43 (Mark 12:35, 36); Matt 19:3–6 (He who … said …); Matt 22:31 (spoken by God); Luke 16:16-17; Luke 18:31; 24: 44-47. Note also that Christ believed in Isaiah's authorship; in David's authorship of Psalm 110; in God's creation of Adam and Eve; in the history of Cain and Abel; in that of Noah and the flood and its results; in the story of Sodom, and of Lot's wife; in the miraculous provision of manna; in the story of the brazen serpent; in Naaman's healing; in the widow of Zarephath; in the story of Jonah etc. There is no doubt that Christ believed implicitly in the authority and inspiration of the Old Testament. It has been rightly said that "the Christian who in his view of the Bible stands on any lower ground than that on which his Lord stood, does so at spiritual peril." It is also interesting to underline the claims Christ made for what He said. He never used the phrase "Thus saith the Lord" as such, but always the direct "I say" etc. Note John 14:26; 16:12–14; Matt 5:22, 28, 32, 34, 39, 44.

c) The New Testament witnesses to the authority of the Old, as well as to itself. Matt 1:22; 2:15; Acts 1:16; 4:25; 28:25; Romans 3:2 (oracles of God); II Tim 3:15–17; Heb 1:5–8, 13; 2:2–4 (through angels; the Lord; confirmed by them that heard etc.); Heb 3:7; 4:4; 12:25, 26; I Peter 1:10–12; II Peter 1:21; Note especially Romans 15:41; I Corinthians 10:11. Also I Corinthians 14:37; I Thessalonians 2:13; II Peter 3:16 Compare verse 2. (Note "as also the other Scriptures.") Rev 22:18–19

IV.   There are also some other ways in which this claim is supported:

a) Whenever and wherever the Holy Spirit is sovereign, He witnesses to the authority and inspiration of God's Word. This is a remarkable fact in both persons and movements in every phase of Church history.

b) The matter of fulfilled prophecy, Messianic and otherwise. E.g. Psalm 22; Isaiah 53; Micah 5:1–5; Zechariah 9:9; Daniel 2; Daniel 7 etc.

c) The unity of the Bible: 66 books, with different human authors, backgrounds, times and even language, yet one theme running throughout. The whole thing is woven together without an editorial committee or any such thing! All 66 books come slowly to be recognized and find their place in the canon of Scripture, e.g. Gen 1–3; Rev 20–22; the book of Revelation, etc.

d) The amazing power inherent within Scripture in all its parts to speak; to change; to convict; to comfort; to create faith; the fact that it speaks to us in a completely contemporary way, etc. What other book has that power?

e) The sobering fact that as soon as man begins to question its authority and full inspiration, belittle its power, or take a superior position to it, that individual opens the floodgates of unbelief, loses his confidence, peace, joy and spiritual life, and gets into an intellectual, albeit religious side water. See II Peter 1:24–25

f) The endurance of God's Word is seen down through the centuries, until we have it in its final form, e.g. Egypt, Judges, the Assyrian and Babylonian Exile, the Roman Conquest and persecutions. We ought also to remember that we all have translations of the Bible, and yet that fact doesn't seem to hinder its power at all. See I Peter 1:24–25.

We are therefore bound to say that as in all other essential matters, e.g. Salvation, the church, His purpose, God has not left the question as to what is and what is not His Word, what is inspired and what is not, what is operative today and what is not, to the tender mercies, or otherwise, or man's own judgement and discretion. He has defined His Word to be received through faith. There are things difficult to understand, things which are hard to reconcile with other things. There are some matters which may appear to us to be incompatible with God. But these difficulties we should expect when the finite starts to touch the Infinite; the imperfect, the perfect; the ignorant, wisdom itself! The created will never fully grasp the Creator!

The amazing fact is that God in the compass of a small volume, in weak human language, had expressed a vast and endless universe of inexhaustible wisdom which century upon century has hardly tapped, and which once trusted and obeyed is powerful enough to change not only individuals, not only nations, but history itself!

And should anyone argue, or still doubt that God could have so spoken to man, then I must ask 'Is God, God?' If He is, then such is gloriously possible, and the basic requirement in us is reverent faith, honest enquiry and true humility. "The fear of the Lord is the beginning of wisdom."

Thus we see the supreme authority of the Word of God. It is like an act of parliament – "operative and authoritative to the last and farthest extremity of its letter."

Conclusion:

The Bible is the result of God breathing out His heart and mind by the Holy Spirit in certain men at different times. It is a God-given revelation of Himself, of His salvation and of His purpose. Herein lays its unique and living authority and power. It is not to be ignored or played with, or argued with, but to be received by faith, in obedience and humility. Human systems will come and go; great men rise and fall; all flesh and all its glory will wither and fall like flowering grass, but the Word of the Lord will endure forever.

Questions

1. State in your own words, what we mean by "Revelation," "Inspiration" and "Authority."

2. Suppose someone said to you, "Why should I believe a book?" What would your answer be?

3. Give five ways in which the Bible claims to have authority. Give examples from Scripture where possible.

4. What verses in the Bible claim that the New Testament is inspired by God?

5. What is the greatest revelation that God has yet made?

6. If someone said to you, "I don't believe the Bible, because it is simply a number of folk tales and stories which have been handed down from Father to son, over many generations," what would your answer be?

7. State some of the dangers which we must avoid as we approach the Bible.

8. What part does the Holy Spirit play in enabling men to make a proper approach to the reading of the Bible?

9. Give reasons why we may accept that the Old Testament has divine authority. Give Scripture references as examples.

10. Give some examples of men, having different personalities, temperaments, etc., whom God has used to give us His Word.

The Bible – The Aim and Scope of the Bible

A. The Bible by Design

The Bible was never designed to cover the whole range of human knowledge in detail, or to be a revelation of all that could be revealed.

It is not a divine encyclopaedia; or a detailed history of the races and nations; or a history book of particular nations. It is not a hand book on Astronomy; Geology; Botany; Zoology, etc. It is not a scientific treatise, nor is it a philosophical treatise. It is not a textbook on theology. If, in fact, it had been any of these, its whole aim would have been seriously obscured if not frustrated, and it would have been unintelligible to the vast majority of mankind. Nevertheless we must say that what the Bible does touch on in any field is absolutely accurate, and has always, in the end, been vindicated.

We must also add that the Bible is not a book of mere sermon outlines, or ideas or illustrations, etc. Nor is it a mere divine promise box, nor "Daily Thoughts," nor a collection of comforting Scriptures. It may contain all these things, but they do not constitute its aim.

Again–it is because the Bible has a definite aim, that it uses "popular" language and modes of thought. Yet it is a remarkable fact that such usage has proved timeless in its value. Thus a child of God in David's time, and in Paul's time, and in Luther's time, and now all can come into the blessing through the same verse! Or a primitive savage and a highly educated man can meet God in an overwhelming way through the same Scripture!

B. Its Aim Governs Its Scope

The Bible has a clearly defined scope, and that scope is governed by its aim.

(See Deut 29:29)

i. We must not expect therefore to find in the Bible what is not important to our understanding of its aim. On the other hand everything which is vitally important to such an understanding is revealed. Its aim governs its scope!

ii. The aim of the Bible is remarkably evidenced in its unity of theme, which once seen is everywhere apparent. The Bible is like an immense tree. Its one life is variously manifested in roots, branches, flowers, leaves, fruit, etc. Every part is livingly connected and essential to the whole! So often as babes in Christ, we see the leaves, or flowers, or branches, but fail to trace the common life and power. We see the parts but not the essential theme.

iii. a) The relationship of Gen 1–3 to Rev 20–22 (See chart on pages 108–109). It is in studying this relationship that we come nearest to understanding the aim of the Bible and therefore its scope.

b) See chart on page 113. Generally speaking we have all the origins, sources, or beginning in Genesis, and the issues, conclusions or fulfillment in Revelation. From Exodus to Jude we have the processes from one to the other.

c) Recognise also how the Bible begins with God, Gen 1:1 and ends with man, Rev 22:21. And its central verses speak of God and man reconciled, Psalm 118:7–9. Note also the first question in the

Old Testament being God's: Gen 3:9, and the first question in the New Testament being man's: Matthew 2:2.

Before we can really see what the theme of the Bible is, we need to note a number of threads which run right through it (see chart on page 139):

• Christ – The promised Seed of the woman, the Messiah.

• Atonement through blood

• God's dwelling place (bride, tabernacle, temple, body, city, etc.– the church)

• God's people–the history of His own from the beginning.

• The adversary of God and the battle of the ages over God's purpose, and His triumph.

Out of all this an essential threefold theme emerges. That theme is ONE Saviour, ONE salvation, and ONE company of the saved. We can put it in different ways–the bringer of salvation; the way of salvation; the saved. Or the Messiah of the covenant; the covenant in His blood; the people of the covenant. Or the Redeemer; the redemption; the redeemed.

Now to understand the aim of the Bible, we must see this threefold theme against the background of God's eternal purpose. (See chart on page 127.) The Bible is a revelation of God's eternal purpose with the supreme aim that we might be saved into it. (See chart on page 128 and page 131.) The scope of the Bible is therefore governed by God's eternal purpose in its immediate and practical application.

C. The Vague or Unmentioned

We must therefore carefully note that much is mentioned only vaguely and much left altogether unmentioned, and in other instances facts are stated without explanation, interpretation or corroboration.

i. What is left out altogether in almost every way e.g. the great Chinese, or Indian Empires. Then what is mentioned only because it touches God's people e.g. Egypt, Persia, Babylon, Greece, Rome. And then what attention is focused upon in a detailed manner e.g. Israel (traced from its source, Abraham!)

ii. Note also the silence of the Bible concerning men like Confucius, Mencius, Motze, Laotz, Buddha, Zoroaster, Plato, Aristotle, etc. Then note the full record of Job, Ruth, Hannah, Samson, etc. Sometimes it would seem that what is insignificant in human eyes is lit up, and what is important in human eyes is only touched upon. The point is that most of the ordinary historical or biographical narrative of Scripture, in so far as it records facts, could have been written by a contemporary historian or biographer, but in the Bible it is interpreted in the light of God's purpose and redemption.

iii. There are also many questions which are either not answered at all or only partly answered, e.g., the origin of sin, Satan! Was there a pre-Adamic race? Are there other inhabited planets? How does God's sovereignty and man's free will tie up? What shall we do in heaven? (Dress, food, sleep, habits, etc.) What does God intend to do once He has built the New Jerusalem? etc., etc.

There are many other questions too, perhaps not so important e.g., what did Christ do between 12–30 years of age, other than being a carpenter? What was He like as a child? What about Moses in his first 80 years? Did Hosea's marriage work out in the end? How did Jeremiah write Lamentations in acrostics and in "kinah" rhythm? Who wrote the Letter to the Hebrews? Did Paul make a mistake in going up to Jerusalem? Was he married, and if so what happened to his wife? Etc., etc.

All these questions and many more are left unanswered in so far as they are not important to our understanding of the Bible's aim.

D. Bible to Reveal

Thus we see that the Bible is a revelation of God's eternal purpose with the aim of our being awakened, saved and incorporated.

We see revealed within its pages:

a) An omnipotent God working according to His own counsel and sovereignly performing His purpose.

b) His eternal purpose–that His Son should head up all things, and be heir of all things, and that a people in union with Him, partaking of the divine nature, should share it all with Him.

c) The foreseeing of the fall and the ruin of man, and the determination of God to save a people out of mankind, and in them and through them to secure His purpose.

d) The appointment of the Son from the beginning to such a saving, keeping and perfecting ministry.

e) His birth among men, "as the seed of the woman" the fulfillment of all prophecy: His sinless life providing the basis for His atoning death; His death on the cross as the Lamb of God, bearing away the sin of the world; and His resurrection and exaltation to the right hand of God, as Lord and Saviour forevermore.

f) The final vindication and triumph of God, His purpose fulfilled, the New Jerusalem, the holy city, the wife of the Lamb, coming down out of heaven, having the glory of God. (See chart on page 139.)

ii. We must note carefully that the Bible is able to make us wise unto salvation through faith, and is able to make us complete, equipped (lit. "fitted out") unto every good work, II Tim 3:15–16. The Bible therefore does not show us merely the way of salvation, nor merely the need to be incorporated into God's purpose. It becomes by the work of the Holy Spirit the practical and powerful means by which all this is accomplished.

iii. We ought also to mention that the Bible is a book of unchanging principles, and once we are saved it is a matter of spiritual education concerning those principles. Heb 4:21; 5:12–6:2. They are vital to our spiritual health and growth.

Questions

1. What is it that governs the scope of the Bible?

2. State in one sentence what is God's eternal purpose?

3. Has God's eternal purpose been altered by the fall?

4. What are the main themes which we find throughout the Bible?

5. Compare Genesis 1–3 with Revelation 20–22. What changes do you see in the following:

    a. The relationship between man and God (Gen 3:8, Rev 21:3)

    b. Mankind itself (i.e. what was man – what has man become)

    c. The effects of the curse

    d. The position of Satan

e. The work and position of the Holy Spirit

6. State briefly what you know of the life of Christ in relation to the eternal purpose of God.

7. Compare the first question in the Old Testament with the first question in the New Testament.

8. What would you say to someone who complained that the Bible is not scientific, and that it is very narrow, telling us very little about history?

9. Describe briefly in your own words, the main phases of God's dealings with man as they are revealed within the scope of Bible.

10. Describe briefly what you have learned about God's dwelling place.

The Structure and Growth of the Bible

The word "Bible came through the Latin from the Greek "Biblia", the Books (note the plural!), by which Greek speaking Christians denoted the Scriptures. Ancient books were written on papyrus or byblos imported from Egypt, and came to be called "Biblion." The use of the plural "Biblia" for the Scripture passed into Latin, where it was treated a singular noun, "the Book". It thus passed into English as "the Bible."

The Bible is in fact both one book and at the same time a library of 66 books. For the most part these 66 books are quite distinct although some were bound together originally as one work, e.g. I & II Samuel and I & II Kings (in LXX 4 books of Kingdom); Ezra and Nehemiah (possibly along with I & II Chronicles); Luke and Acts; possibly Judges and Ruth. The period during which they were written covers not less than 1,500 years, the New Testament being confined to about the last 100 years of that time. The books were written over quite a large area, ranging from Italy in the West, to Persia and Mesopotamia in the East. The writers were not only parted by time and place, but were greatly diverse in background. There were kings, priests, prophets, shepherds, peasants, fisherman, statesmen, soldiers, courtiers, at least one doctor of medicine, and one of law and one ex-tax collector!

Then, too, we find every kind of literary method used from biography, personal memoirs and diaries, correspondence, to poetry, parable and allegory, prophecy and clear dogmatic teaching. It is truly a library, and yet with all its diversity, there is a unity from beginning to end. True it is not the apparent technical unity of a machine, but rather the living unity of a plant or organism. Nor is this unity the product and work of a human anthologist, a compiler or editor, but somehow over the centuries of time it has grown until it has reached what we now know as the Bible.

These 66 books are divided into two unequal halves–39 in the first division which we commonly call the Old Testament, and 27 in the second, which we commonly call the New Testament.

A. The Old and New Testaments

The word "Testament" came to be used of this major two fold division of the Bible, due to a mistranslation of a Greek word which meant: arrangement, disposition, testament or will, covenant or poet.

In the LXX version, the oldest translation of the Old Testament into Greek, this Greek word was used to translate the Hebrew word for "Covenant," and was thus understood by all readers of the Greek Old Testament. It is interesting to note that there was another Greek word meaning "covenant" or "pact" but the LXX translators rejected it because it suggested a pact between equals, whereas the former Greek word was better suited to the Biblical idea of "covenant" – God's pact with His people freely made by Him in sovereign grace. When the LXX was translated into Latin (from whence the Latin Vulgate), two words vied for the honour of translating the Greek word used for "covenant"–"TESTAMENTUM" (meaning last will and testament) favoured by European scholars, because they seemingly did not understand the second meaning of the Greek word: "INSTRUMENTUM" (meaning legal and binding agreement or document) favoured by African scholars.

In the end, Europe won and the word "Testamentum" was used and thus passed in the English as "Testament." It would have been interesting if the word "Instrumentum" had won, and we had in English "The Old Instrument and The New Instrument."

The use of the word "testament" is in many ways misleading, for most people, if they understand it at all, do NOT understand it as the books of expressing the Old Covenant, and those expressing the New, but rather as a last will and testament. It is important for us to understand this word "Covenant," since it is used to cover the whole Bible. It is unfortunate that in the AV the word "Covenant" appears in the Old Testament and "Testament" largely appears in the New. The Revised and modern versions have translated it uniformly as "Covenant," see Gen 9:9, 16; 15:8–10, 17–21; Exodus 24:3–8; Jeremiah 31:31–34; Matt 26:28; I Cor 11:25; II Cor 3:6; Heb 7:22.

The Biblical sense of "Covenant" means a solemn pact or agreement initiated by God in His love and grace, freely bestowed upon us, and ratified by the shedding of precious blood and death. By this He promises to save, redeem, forgive, and share His life and gifts. It has the sense of mutual belonging; a kind of marriage bond and relationship; an incorporation into God's family and household.

Thus the 39 books of the Old, PREPATORY Covenant illustrate and explain God's ways with His own, leading up and pointing to the NEW and ETERNAL Covenant, expressed and explained in the last 27 books. Now many will ask, "Do we really need the Old Covenant when we have the New? Has it not been rendered completely obsolete?" We have to remember that the whole Old Testament is vital preparation and foundation for the New Testament. The Bible for the Lord Jesus, the apostles, and the early church literally consisted exclusively of the books of the Old

Covenant. All that we have in the New flowered and fruited on the stock of the Old.

Remember:

The New is in The Old contained. The Old is in The New explained.

The New is in The Old concealed. The Old is in The New revealed.

The New is in The Old enfolded. The Old is in The New unfolded.

In our studies "The Aim and Scope of the Bible" we have already pointed out the threefold theme in the Scriptures. This theme binds both Old and New together:

a.) The Mediator of the Covenant.

Matt 1:1–17; Luke 3:23–38; Heb 8:6; 1 Tim 2:5.

The Messiah is the focal point of the Old; the Saviour of the New–the Messiah Saviour is the heart of all.

1. Luke 24:27, 44–45
2. How immeasurably poorer we would be without Messianic prophecies, e.g. Gen 3:15; Psalm 22; Isaiah 53, etc, etc.
3. Also the prophecies of His coming glory and Kingdom–cf. Isaiah, Ezekiel, Micah, Daniel, etc., etc.
4. Think of 1 Chronicles 1–9 consisting of genealogies. They are nothing in themselves. Yet they are part of the authentication of Christ as the seed of the woman, the seed of Abraham, the seed of David.
5. Could we really understand His priesthood without the Old Testament?

b.) The Covenant in His blood Rev 5:6

John 1:29. The title "Lamb of God" carried great meaning to the Jewish hearers. It meant to them sacrifice for sin, the Passover deliverance and redemption; Matt 26:28 (Passover). The Lamb slain, precious blood being shed, is foundational through both Old and New.

1. How could we understand the atonement without the Old Testament and especially the offerings? See Leviticus.

2. What would we understand by "Covenant in His Blood" without the Old Testament?

3. How could we understand the blood of Christ – its cleansing, covering and "making nigh" power without the illustrations of the Old Testament?

c.) The People of the Covenant

Heb 11: esp. 39–40 Acts 7:38 op. Heb 2:12. In the LXX the Greek word "Ekklesia," used in New Testament for "church," is used for the Hebrew word, "kahal," translated "congregation" in the AV, RV thus the Early Church, which used the LXX version of the Old Testament saw that it was one company of the redeemed in Old and New.

1. Heb 11:10 cf 12:22–24; Rev 21:12, 14 (12 Tribes, 12 Apostles)

2. Gal 3:7; 6:16

3. Eph 2:11–14

4. I Cor 10:1–11

IV. Without the Old Covenant we are in grave danger of misunderstanding many things, or at least not having a balanced understanding. Nearly every major Biblical idea or conception finds its origin within the Old.

V. We also need the Old Testament in other ways. For example, to understand the book of Revelation we need an understanding of Ezekiel, Daniel, Zechariah, and Malachi. Indeed, without the Old Testament the symbols figures and types used in the New have little meaning or are open to misinterpretation.

B. The Arrangement of the Books

There are three main arrangements of the books – the Hebrew: the LXX or Hellenist; the final or Christian. The whole subject of the way in which the various books came to occupy their final positions is fascinating. We will deal firstly with the Hebrew arrangement and then the LXX and final arrangement together. We ought to note that within these main arrangements there was a good deal of variation

The Hebrew Arrangement of the Books of the Old Covenant

a) The Law (Torah) Gen, Exodus, Leviticus, Numbers, Deuteronomy

b) The Prophets (Nevi'im) subdivided:

- The Former; Joshua, Judges, Samuel, Kings
- The Latter; Isaiah, Jeremiah, Ezekiel, the 12 minor prophets.

c) The Writings (Kethuvim) Subdivided:

- Psalms, Proverbs, Job
- The Five Scrolls (Megilloth), Song of Songs, Ruth, lamentations, Ecclesiastes, Esther
- Daniel, Ezra-Nehemiah, Chronicles

a) How did this three-fold Hebrew division of the Old Testament take place? We cannot with any certainty state its origin! It is often suggested that it represents the stages of growth in the Hebrew Bible, and its recognition part by part as canonical. We shall say more about this later.

b) It is interesting to note that roughly we have here in the first five books–the nucleus of Old Testament faith; in the second division, objective expansion and interpretation of the first; in the third, subjective expansion and interpretation.

c) We can however say that the Law, the first five books, called by the Jews "The Five Fifths" were associated in their main body with one another from an early date, and were the first to be recognized. There seems to have been no variation in the order of the books

d) The second division, the prophets, is interesting since it contains a large amount of history i.e. the former prophets. These books were not included merely because prophets were responsible for their writing, but because it was history interpreted. This is true of Joshua to Kings. The latter Prophets contain prophecy as generally understood. The main point of interest here is the exclusion of Daniel, and the gathering of the twelve books into one book. We should also note that there was a certain amount of variation in order of books in the latter prophets.

e) The third division, the writings, is a little more difficult to understand. It seems to be almost miscellaneous. This division had the greatest variation in the order of its books. We give the most general and accepted above. We can understand the Psalms (the hymnal of Old Testament church,) Proverbs and Job, being put together, as also the five scrolls, so called, because one of them was read at each of the great festivals (in order: Passover, Pentecost, the anniversary of Jerusalem's destruction, the feast of Tabernacles, and Purim). It is not so easy to understand why Daniel is here, nor why Ezra, Nehemiah, Chronicles, in that quite unchronological order!! One feels that there must be spiritual meaning behind it.

iii. The Final Arrangement (LXX and Christian) of the books of both Old and New Covenants.

a) The Old Covenant

The Pentateuch: Gen. Exod, Lev, Num, Deut

The Historical Books: Josh, Judges, Ruth, I & II Samuel, I & II Kings, I & II Chronicles, Ezra, Nehemiah, Esther. The poetical books Job, Psalms, Proverbs, Ecclesiastes, Song of Songs.

The prophetical books: Isaiah, Jeremiah, Lamentations, Ezekiel, Daniel, the twelve (Hosea – Malachi).

Note: The Final arrangement of the Old Testament came to us via LXX and Latin Vulgate. The LXX or Hellenist arrangement was a roughly chronological one. Whether it was based on older arrangements we cannot dogmatically state. In this rearrangement of the Hebrew Bible, there were many variations, but it finally resolved itself into the arrangement we have today. We must note Ruth's place with Judges, Chronicles, Ezra-Nehemiah, Esther, at the end of Kings is an approximate chronological order Lamentations is added to Jeremiah; and Daniel to the Major Prophets.

b) The New Covenant:

The Gospels Matthew, Mark, Luke, John

The historical Acts

The Didactical Romans, I & II Corinthians, Gal, Eph, Phil, Col, I & II Thess, I & II Tim, Titus, Philemon, Heb, James, I & II Peter, I, II & III John, Jude

The Prophetical Revelation

a) The 27 books of the New Testament consist of five narrative books, twenty-one letters (personal or treatises), and one book of visions. The four-fold division corresponds in some ways with the Old Covenant.

b) How did the arrangement come about? The individual Gospels were originally circulating on their own various locations. Mark, Peter's young companion, put the gospel preached by Peter into writing at Rome; Matthew circulated in Palestine and was based largely on collections of the Lord's sayings; Luke wrote a two volume history for Gentiles–Luke and Acts. These were bound in one at the beginning. It probably has in it much of the Gospel as Paul preached it. At the end of the 1st Century John writes his Gospel, when the others were already circulating.

By the beginning of the 2nd century the four Gospels were brought together, and an amazing four-fold picture of Christ emerged. When this happened Acts was separated from Luke and circulated on its own, or sometimes with the general letters (James, I & II Peter, Jude)

Paul's letters were at first kept by churches or individuals to whom they were addressed, but by the end of the 1st century they had been collected together under one cover and entitled "The Apostle."

Gradually these collections came together and the arrangement we have now grew. Revelation and Hebrews were the two major works over which there was much discussion, along with some of the small letters, and it was not until the 4th Century that they were finally given universal recognition. As the collection grew there was much variation in the order in which books or letters appeared. Nowhere is this clearer than in Revelation, which occupied various positions other than the final one for some centuries. The Apostle John did not write it as a conclusion, for there was no New Testament to conclude at that point! It was under God's hand that it was placed at the conclusion of the Bible. And this is also true of the final positioning of all the other books.

C. The Canon of Scripture

We have now covered something of the growth of the Bible and the arrangement of the books. Now we must ask how was it decided which books should be included. Who made so solemn a decision and when? It is over this question that we use the word "canon." All those books included we call "canonical," and those excluded, "apocryphal."

The word "canon" came to us through Latin and Greek from a Semitic word "kaneh" meaning "read" (from which we get the English word "cane" then "canal" and "channel," etc.) and because of its use by the ancient world for measuring, it came to mean "measuring rod" or carpenter's rule. It seems to be applied not only to that which measures, but that which is measured.

It thus has two meanings:

1. An index, list or catalogue–a certain group or number comprising something.
2. A rule, standard, law. The value and authority contained within those things.

By the 4th Century it had come to be applied to the Bible, which had arrived at its conclusive arrangement. The term covered not only the list of the books recognized as inspired which comprised it, but the authority of those books above all others. They were recognized as supremely authoritative for faith and life. We must be clear that the books of the Bible have not become authoritative because they are canonical. They are canonical because over the years they have been universally recognized as possessing divine authority. We should also point out that no church councils, or other groups, "canonized" Scripture. They merely recognized what was already acknowledged over many years and in wide circles.

The Canon of the Old Covenant

a) The process was a long and gradual one. It would seem reasonable that it followed approximately the line of the Hebrew arrangement, although we have no definite authority for this. Certainly by our Lord's time the Old Covenant was complete. See Luke 24:44.

(Note Luke 11:51 cf. Matt 23:35. Abel – Zechariah. See Gen 4:8; II Chronicles 24:21).

It seems quite clear that our Lord, the apostles and the early church viewed the Old Testament in its Hebrew arrangement as divinely authoritative and inspired. Indeed, we must add that from the very beginning it would seem that the books, which now comprise our Old Testament, were recognized as such. The very fact of debate as to whether the widely held view that they were divinely inspired was valid.

b) Let us consider these three main divisions:

1. The law, from the very beginning, the Pentateuch, was recognized as THE Word of God. It was the first part to be officially recognized, probably at an early date, and with little if any controversy.

2. The prophets, the two main divisions of Hebrew Bible, were recognized for the most part, it would seem, by Ezra's time (mid–5th Century BC). By 2nd Century BC they were fully recognized, although over Ezekiel there was much debate (due to his involved visions and difficulty in reconciling Ezekiel 40–48 with the Pentateuch regulations)!

3. The writings—it is over this division we have the greatest difficulty. It seems certain that by our Lord's time, it was officially recognized, and in all probability much earlier. Yet as late as 70 AD there was heated debate about Esther (it seemed so pagan), Ecclesiastes (not very orthodox), Canticles (Song of Songs) and Proverbs. It is interesting to note that the conclusion of these debates was the absolute recognition of all these books as canonical.

4. Apocryphal writings, although viewed in many cases as valuable, have never been accorded by the Rabbis the same recognition as the canonical books. It was the uniform tradition of the Jews that Malachi ended the prophetic and scriptural inspiration.

The LXX included a number of these apocryphal writings, and although they were included, Greek-speaking Jews never mixed them up with the canonical. When however, Greek-speaking Gentile Christians began to read the LXX they tended to accept the whole as Scripture, making no distinction. Jerome, the greatest scholar amongst the church fathers, was the one who clearly defined the difference. In fact, it is to him we owe the term "apocryphal books." Nevertheless, the Roman Catholic Church finally accepted a number of these books as canonical, which the Reformers and Protestants refused to do.

We must however say this—that while there has been universal recognition of 39 books, which comprise the Old Testament from an early date, there has never been anywhere a unanimous verdict on the Apocrypha.

The Canon of the New Covenant

a) The process of the New Testament canon was again a gradual one, though not as long as the Old Testament. Nearly all the New Testament as we now have it, was written by the end of the 1st Century.

b) The Lord Himself had promised that the Holy Spirit would lead the apostles in all truth, John 14:26; 16:12–15. Note in the New Testament:

Past: Gospels

Present: Acts - Jude

Future: Revelation

These were all the written deposit of the Truth.

c) By 140 AD the Gospels, Acts and Apostle (writings of Paul), were recognized as divinely inspired and authoritative, with one exception, to be placed alongside the Old Testament canon. See II Peter 3:15–16. This meant 18 books out of 27 were considered canonical. Only John's Gospel caused some dispute toward the end of 2nd Century. But after that it was universally accepted. It was about that time that these books were first called the New Testament (by Tertullian).

d) By 230 AD only Hebrews, II Peter, I, II & III John, James and Jude were disputed along with some apocryphal literature that some would have included (epistle of Barnabus, the shepherd of Hermes, Didache). Revelation was more or less generally accepted by then.

e) By the 4th Century the 27 books of New Testament as we now have it were universally recognized. (3rd Synod of Carthage 397 AD). It was this stated "besides the canonical Scriptures nothing was to be read in the Church under the title of 'The Divine Scriptures'."

f) It is clear that the apostolic authorship counted much with the early church in its recognition of these books. This is the reason for the flood of New Testament apocryphal literature under apostolic names. It is interesting to see that the Church gradually sifted and sorted out what was divinely inspired from what was not. All scholarship agrees that the literature is nowhere near the New Testament standard.

Conclusion

Now let us summarise this whole matter: the canon of Scripture grew over many, many years, and was searchingly selective. No religious body or council "made Scripture" or canonized books." They simply officially acknowledged what was universally recognized already. To this we must ask the inward testimony of the Holy Spirit in the Church and in the individual not only then, nor subsequently, but now, to the divine authority of these books. Indeed the supreme wonder must be the oversight of the Holy Spirit in the whole process of the Bible's formation from beginning to end!

Questions

1. State briefly why we need the Old Testament to have a proper understanding of the New Testament.

2. What is the Biblical meaning of the word "covenant"? Why is it that there is misunderstanding about the real meaning of the original word, meaning covenant?

3. Describe briefly the Hebrew arrangement of the Books of the Old Covenant.

4. Describe the final arrangement of the New Covenant, and how it came about.

5. Why is it that the four Gospels are so remarkable?

6. Write a couple of sentences on the part played by the writings of the Apostle Paul in the New Testament.

7. How did the books of the Old Testament reach their final arrangement?

8. What is the meaning of the term "canon"? Trace the growth of this meaning.

9. State in your own words what you know about "The Apocrypha."

10. Write a paragraph on the canonicity of the New Testament.

www.ingramcontent.com/pod-product-compliance
Lightning Source LLC
Chambersburg PA
CBHW072341090426
42741CB00012B/2879